Why Conservatism Failed

(And How To Save It)

By Martin Goldberg

Copyright 2023

Dedication

To Beatriz, for your bountiful kindness and undying friendship.

Table of Contents

I. Introduction

"Together, we will make America strong again. We will make America wealthy again. We will make America proud again. We will make America safe again, And yes, together, we will make we will make America great again."

These were the words of Donald Trump immediately after he took the presidential oath of office on January 20th, 2017. For the first time in ten years, there was good reason for political conservatives to be hopeful. Unified government had returned to their column, this time unbridled by the excessive influence of those war-hungry interventionists who dominated the Bush Administration. Perhaps now, following years of Tea Party wrangling and dismay over weak, moderate Republicans, something could actually change. Conservatism was about to have its glorious moment in God's Sun.

But things didn't turn out that way. Trump governed across a tempestuous four years, battling intraparty opposition and the wrath of a vengeful press corps, notching the occasional win while scarcely moving the needle towards that idealized state which his supporters had so long awaited. By the end of his term, government spending was at historic highs, corporate interests sat coddled in their usual comfort, a Leftist administration was delightfully inbound, and hundreds of conservative supporters were facing the fury of a politicized Justice Department. Conservatism, again given a chance to triumph, had elected for the tradition of failure.

For many right-wingers, the answer to this added disappointment was devolution into prototypical gnashing of teeth about "RINO" politicians, or the ominous "Deep State", both reminiscent of M. Stanton Evans' classic observation that, "By the time they get into a position where they can help us, they are no longer one of us."[1] Others claimed the problem prevailed due to violent and uncompromising liberal opposition.

They are all correct – and just as swiftly – completely wrong. In reality, the blamed factors preventing a competent and far-reaching conservative movement from attaining major policy success are actually control components of the ideology itself, and deeper historical traditions. We can no more indict fair-weather moderates for conservative failures than insist radicals are at fault; both share guilt on account of *how* their philosophy operates. Thus a continued lack of structural reform to the vision will lead to victory being unsuccessful, making allegiance to the cause somewhat despairing.

As matters stand today, Conservatism has failed because the concept so prides itself in not doing much more than existing state maintenance, like a demissionary prime minister in one of the routine, outgoing European governments. Such political strategies align with William F. Buckley's description of a conservative as one who, "stands athwart history, yelling Stop", but otherwise pushing delay over belief, soft contentment instead of a vision for change. It explains the nuances and proclivities of modern conservatives as much as those in prior ages, where doing little was viewed to be an impressive act. Their seeming incapacity to deliver thus becomes gloriously justified, for at the heart is nothing more than devotion and comfort towards protecting some vague and recent past, but only to a very limited degree. As Benjamin Disraeli summarized brilliantly in his novel *Coningsby*:

> "There was indeed a considerable shouting about what they called Conservative principles; but the awkward question naturally arose, what will you conserve? The prerogatives of the Crown, provided they are not exercised; the independence of the House of Lords, provided it is not asserted; the Ecclesiastical estate, provided it is regulated by a commission of laymen. Everything, in short, that is established, as long as it is a phrase and not a fact.

> In the meantime, while forms and phrases are religiously cherished in order to make the semblance of a creed, the rule of practice is to bend to the passion or combination of the hour. Conservatism assumes in theory that everything established should be maintained; but adopts in practice that everything that is established is indefensible. To reconcile this theory and this practice, they produce what they call 'the best bargain;' some arrangement which has no principle and no purpose, except to obtain a temporary lull of agitation, until the mind of the Conservatives, without a guide and without an aim, distracted, tempted, and bewildered, is prepared for another arrangement, equally statesmanlike with the preceding one. [...]

> Conservatism was an attempt to carry on affairs by substituting the fulfilment of the duties of office for the performance of the functions of government; and to maintain this negative system by the mere influence of property, reputable private conduct, and what are called good connections. Conservatism discards Prescription, shrinks from Principle, disavows Progress; having rejected all respect for Antiquity, it offers no redress for the Present, and makes no preparation for the Future."[2]

Of course while Disraeli's characterization may be quite accurate, its utilization here will not prevent detractors from appealing to ideological purism based on their specific school of Rightist politics, such as libertarianism or paleoconservatism. These nuances shall be at various junctions acknowledged, yet the extent to which they appear does not somehow counterman a common thread of failures running through the right-wing philosophical community. Furthermore, excessive concessions to the purists are unwarranted because power is ultimately exercised through political movements, their financial supporters, and organs of the state. Hence the claimed perfection of a particular viewpoint is irrelevant if it cannot be transformed into credible policy for the nation. Consequently, this book will concentrate on political developments, with a heavy bias favoring American politics and the Republican Party's bouts with public administration. Since relevant iterations in this regard have been under the auspices of the second "New Right" school that solidified during Ronald Reagan's presidency, our focus will be largely on its achievements and shortcomings. The inherent advantage is an empowerment of rank-and-file conservatives to assess what has gone wrong, and also explain how defeats might be nursed towards national rejuvenation.

Good consideration insists that a few points are clarified before we continue. For one, the goal here is not to deliberate on an excessive history of conservative movements outside the American context. Such works exist, yet they are less concerned with the proactive now than distant chronological enterprises. Furthermore, I will make use of the terms "Conservatism" and the "Plural Right" in a roughly interchangeable manner, referring to the collective, majority actions of the philosophical movement tethered to the second New Right and its associated Republican Party. The term "conservative" is to be used in reference to particular right-wing sentiments, or in pluralized form movement backers themselves. Sporadic use of "Rightist" or "right-wing" will add diversity to this equation, though still signaling the territory of the Reagan-established New Right coalition. On a similar note, the term "Plural Left" shall be employed to reference the broader array of media forces, public advocates, and political denizens aligned with the Democratic Party.

The book is designed to begin with the critical flaws of philosophy contributing to Conservatism's underperformance, at times bleeding them into more specific policy matters where missed opportunities have abounded. The greater issues will be examined to pinpoint a historical pattern of concessions that steadily render any firm right-wing agenda neutered by the establishment. Finally, we must assess what might be done to salvage conservative values using the constitutional system birthed by the Founding Era.

II. History and Philosophical Concern

As part of creating a causeway across the river of disinformation, it is necessary to look at the roots and development of Conservatism. We could obviously go back to a depiction of the "conservative" monarchs of old, who preciously guarded their own power and the aristocracy, at times through the violation of yet-unrecognized individual rights for their detractors. American Conservatism plays a tricky game however because it came about in the shambles of revolution *against* the established monarchy of George III. Conservatives since the Founding have purported to defend the freedoms codified by that larger revolt of (classical) liberalism against British hegemony, albeit with differing interpretations and policy proposals.

In point, historical Rightists often vacillated on the matter of America's destiny, with some preferring a weakened federal administration and stronger states' rights, while others saw a robust national government as essential to developing industry and trade power. The former group typically occupied specific factions among the agrarian nation-aspiring Democratic-Republicans, while others endorsed the nationalistic American System of high tariffs and central banking. Their varied positions would come to a head amid the slavery crisis and Civil War, when Abraham Lincoln invaded the emerging Confederacy to protect his interpretation of the federal union.

The post-Lincoln conservative movement found itself divided along a somewhat complex array of ideological lines. While moderate factions still professed a skittishness towards diminishing states' rights, the Radical Republican orientation of certain national leaders led to a slew of federal legislation extending Reconstruction oversight to the South and reaffirming the aggressive unionism of the earlier conflict. Such muscular conservatives did move to combat abortion and the proliferation of prostitution nationally, but their association with big business corruption under the presidency of Ulysses Grant kindled an elitist image that would only solidify in the coming decades.

Although imperfect, Grant did christen some of the anti-corruption efforts that would color a left-wing populist faction of the GOP during the early 1900s. Such progressives were no doubt inspired by the recent experiences of the Gilded Age, when the American economy expanded dramatically to the benefit of some, while millions of others were remanded to poverty and homelessness. It was through the championing of policies like Teddy Roosevelt's "Square Deal" that Republicans worked to enact a modern regulatory state, although not with the level of corporate pain that one might assume. According to Gabriel Kolko, policymakers in the Progressive Era actually worked closely with the captains of industry to create regulations which ultimately benefited large corporations and their system of profit accumulation.[3] From this point we may generate criticism of regulation (and its potential for capture) from the libertarian corners of the Plural Right; what remains more important is that a pro-business slant continued almost unhindered within the conservative movement from this point forward.

The Tripartite Split

Despite the rise of progressive Republicans, traditionalist conservatives focused on limiting government and adhering to classically liberal, laissez-faire economic policies during the 1910s and 1920s. Followers of these "Old Right" principles helped stave off American engagement on an internationalist basis, contributing to the coalition that defeated the League of Nations treaty because it stood to usurp war declaration powers from Congress. Pro-business reforms and tax cuts were approved under the presidencies of Warren Harding and Calvin Coolidge, further endorsing the GOP's association with a defense of industry leaders and the upper echelons of society. These approaches would be largely followed by Herbert Hoover until the great collapse in 1929 pushed him towards protectionist measures and increased government oversight for the agricultural sector.

Where we begin to see the modern divide which highlights Conservatism's decline is the tempestuous 1940s. By this point the Democratic Party had established itself as a dominant political force, both in terms of responding to the Great Depression with the New Deal and joining the Allies in a global war against Axis states. Traditional conservative voices like "Mr. Republican" Senator Robert Taft of Ohio maintained the isolationist line, campaigning against intervention before the attack on Pearl Harbor, opposing the internment of Japanese-Americans, and expressing skepticism towards the post-war NATO alliance.

While Taft kept the political faith, a new crop of conservatives were ascending who perceived politics in different terms. Rather than maintaining a fierce hostility towards the state, these actors viewed the contours of Leftist institutions and welfare programs to be essentially "settled government", unworthy of debate apart from the occasional moderate reform or redirection. They coincided with the development of what James Burnham termed the "managerial revolution", wherein a class of dominant bureaucratic liberal overseers in management, business, and the media would displace prior bourgeois elites in terms of political influence. The emerging ideological wave destined to become known as neoconservatism did not attempt to repeal the ensconced structures of the post-New Deal consensus on government, but rather sought to "conservatize" those establishments using right-wing ideas.[4] According to Irving Kristol, the movement's unquestionable godfather, their perspective worked as follows:

> "In economic and social policy, it [neoconservatism] feels no lingering hostility to the welfare state, nor does it accept it resignedly, as a necessary evil. Instead it seeks not to dismantle the welfare state in the name of free market economics but rather to reshape it so as to attach to it the *conservative* predispositions of the people. This reshaping will presumably take the form of trying to rid the welfare state of its paternalistic orientation, imposed on it by Left-liberalism, and making it into the kind of 'social insurance state' that provides the social and economic security a modern citizenry demands while minimizing government intrusion into individual liberties."[5]

Voices like Kristol were also adamant about maintaining the international presence of the United States as a military power. During the 1940s campaign period, eastern liberal Republicans more readily aligned with the interventionist stances of FDR worked to undermine the presidential hopes of the aforementioned Senator Taft, anointing instead the pro-New Deal Wendell Wilkie in 1940, and two iterations of Governor Thomas Dewey in 1944 and 1948.[6] Dwight Eisenhower's election in 1952 provided a partial victory for the neoconservatives, but his health troubles led some to attempt a removal of the right-wing Richard Nixon as vice presidential candidate in 1956, fearing the latter might assume power upon Eisenhower's death.[7] Although Nixon ran in 1960, it was on the basis of a compromise platform which won the approval of the Leftist New York governor Nelson Rockefeller.[8] Four years later, Rockefeller intervened to damage the nomination of Senator Barry Goldwater, likening the Arizona legislator's supporters to Nazis and communists at the Republican National Convention.[9] This event is critical to note because Goldwater represented a loose coalition of individuals who made up the first "New Right", a group dedicated to opposing communism globally, but also defending traditionalist perspectives on the role of government in everyday life.

With Goldwater's electoral demise in 1964 and Nixon's fairly liberal, aborted presidency spanning 1969-1974, Conservatism was largely shed of its philosophical origins on a national level at least until the 1980 triumph of Ronald Reagan, who championed what became known as the second "New Right". Though Reagan embodied a *symbolic* restoration of the values advanced by Calvin Coolidge and Barry Goldwater, his administration was in fact quite tame, achieving some economic wins but largely disappointing the fiscal restraint and social fronts long-heralded by conservatives. Reagan continued the Plural Right's journey towards a neoconservative foreign policy with his aggressive participation in proxy wars across the globe, including support for counterrevolutionary forces fighting Soviet-backed rebels in the Americas, and Operation Cyclone, a massive arming program benefiting Islamic radicals opposed to communism in

Afghanistan. He would further grant amnesty to nearly three million illegal immigrants with the 1986 Immigration Reform and Control Act, an effort that was continued by his more moderate successor, George H.W. Bush, who expanded legal immigration with legislation in 1990. Bush is of course well-known for his spearheading of the Gulf War against Iraq and declaration of a "New World Order", something his son George W. Bush built on through the invasion of Afghanistan in 2001, and Iraq during 2003.

It is important to remark that yet another faction in the conservative movement was identified leading up to and succeeding the Reagan years. According to the late writer Samuel Francis, a subgroup described as "Middle American Radicals" emerged during the 1970s to reject not only the march away from older conservative values, but also centralization of power by neoconservative elites and their acceptance of government largesse.[10] Such Americans formed an alliance of sorts with the Reagan coalition in hopes of localizing and privatizing government, though these goals did not materialize in any significant way during the Reagan or Bush presidencies.

To appreciate why the hopes of traditional conservatives are so often dashed by political dynamics, we must look at the integral values of the philosophy itself. Although somewhat dusty and unappealing to the darting mind, they provide a window into why precisely achieving any substantial reform on the national front is difficult, if not completely impossible.

III. The Liberal Individualism Pact

At the heart of any discussion about Conservatism as a philosophy will be its relationship to liberalism, which often seems to materialize as the senior partner in a historical coalition of thought. America was after all founded on the basis of a classically liberal, Enlightenment-inspired revolution *against* the traditional aristocracy and monarchy of Britain. For context, old-style Tories in England defended this royal system, embodying a form of rigid, hierarchical politics,[11] while their Whig opponents pushed reformist schemes incorporating both liberal values and the conservative mores we see descended to politics today. Keeping with their general skepticism towards the Crown, the Founders enshrined in the Constitution an assembly of principles and protections (in a negative sense of rights), to guard against the threats of an imperious royalty (or state). Over time however the liberal reformers ascribed to various parts of American history agitated for expanded protections favoring disenfranchised groups, along with larger government programs to serve them.

Faced with these shifting foundations, conservative advocates had to carefully choose how they might proceed in defending the traditions of America's past. Some actors elected for a staunch elitist front, insisting on evading attempts to dislodge the plantation owner aristocracy of the Old South, and its native belief in strong states' rights. Others agreed with a more powerful role for the federal government, and determined that decisive action was required to liberate subjugated classes from slavery. The latter coalition would support Abraham Lincoln's aggressive move to crush Southern separatism during the Civil War, resulting in an immensely dominant federal structure and comparatively neutered state administrations. In the case of both factions, they believed themselves to be guarding the individual rights assured by the Constitution, albeit from different perspectives entirely. Moreover, those conservatives skeptical of federal intervention to ensure rights have been succeeded by figures typically in agreement with the idea.

This captivation with rights for the individual becomes of essence as we see the fundamental crisis of conservative thought: how can one go about securing societal order based on the values of a collectively-held past when the highest ideal is interpreted to be self-liberation by free and independent souls? The answer holds grim provisions for those failing to expect them. While fostering creativity and freedom can allow people to experience fulfilling lives unbridled by top-down coercion, those elements open the door to narcissistic deconstruction of the most seminal social rules and principles. An evident example of this would be LGBTQ culture. Even the most libertarian conservatives of earlier eras would have at best allowed for "live and let die" attitudes towards the non-straight population, assuming them to be content with their respective communities and private lives. What they did not anticipate was individualism reaching a fever pitch to where people would attempt to redefine their gender (and compel the pronoun language of others), serving a personal quest for validation and comfort. The fact that conservatives generally embraced individualistic trends while largely neglecting the stronger social (and at times governmental) controls required to maintain order make them complicit in this modern façade of experimental chaos affecting the nation.

Able Rightists might object here by suggesting enough freedoms have been entrenched, and hence the demands of the present social justice communities are out of hand.[12] But who is to say they are excessive? After all, liberalism thrives off the idea of continual progress, unstoppable betterment, the curing of all social ills impacting the altar of the individual. Or, in the words of the renowned economist Friedrich Hayek, it is a philosophical system which makes the individual, "the ultimate judge of his ends".[13] To stop at one junction because it sates the nerves of the present conservative column makes little sense, particularly if the individual remains a high virtue. Conservatism has for the most part co-opted earlier liberal reforms to its "now sacred" standard, so why should anything less be expected in the new era of radicalism? As one author notes, "If everything is an individual's private choice, there remains little opportunity to teach, to positively shape, or even simply to question preferences that do, in fact, deserve scrutiny. By pretending there is no system connecting us, we give up the opportunity to correct it."[14] Similarly, the writer W.H. Auden noted that excessive freedom under liberalism simply leads to emptiness and a search for meaning in the form of more hamster-wheel liberation:

> "Emancipated from the traditional beliefs of a closed society, he can no longer believe simply because his forefathers did and he cannot imagine not believing—he has found no source or principle of direction to replace them. [...] Liberalism is at a loss to know how to handle him, for the only thing liberalism knows to offer is more freedom, and it is precisely freedom in the sense of lack of necessity that is his trouble."[15]

The popular YouTuber Academic Agent has highlighted this exact social crisis by describing Western political culture as operating on the basis of a post-1960s assumption that the highest social ideal is liberation of individuals along personal (and often sexual) grounds.[16] While marketed ostensibly as freedom, the cultural fixation has only morphed and grown, used as an effective tool to make hammer blows against what foundational cornerstones support civilization. The early drive for sexual autonomy brought on by the counterculture and contraceptive pill were useful for Leftist radicals because they destroyed any shining imperative to form families. Women had little reason to "settle down", as pregnancy could be readily delayed, allowing for longer years of guiltless love-making and career-chasing to the heart's content. Such rampant narcissism made men equally unlikely to take relationships seriously in an environment where they possess the ability to gain higher "notch counts" absent the risk of financial responsibilities. Even further potential for accountability was wiped away with the lavish growth of government welfare programs, which foster the delusional belief that people can be "fully liberated" from a dastardly conservative establishment. According to Peter Hitchens, the rise of government did away with a need for family, as the state became a fallback for those confident in their libertine emancipation.[17]

Some on the Right will address this by advocating for reductions in welfare or government spending. A reasonable take, perhaps, but it does not explain *why* we have reached the point where such programs exist, despite the assumed effectiveness of the freedom-based approach. Did individuals collectively agitate for more government because they hated liberty itself, or might their actions be a strange furtherance of it, albeit along convoluted lines? The fact remains, certain government programs allow people to live to the greatest extents of their base desires, sans the onerous weight of accepting whichever consequences arise. Perhaps a simpler explanation may ride in sequence with Auden's theory, where fathers pass on an inheritance of freedom and prosperity to their children, but are hated for it.[18]

As the astute are already aware, a culture grounded in such individualistic notions is bound to become unstable. Edmund Burke pointedly observed that a society which dilutes social membership by emphasizing the lone person over community and nation would be broken down into the, "dust and powder of individuality."[19] Following in his footsteps, Russell Kirk employed the work of Robert Nisbet to demonstrate a classical conservative view of individualism actually coming *after* various cultural pillars:

> "The family, religious association, and local community—these, the conservatives insisted, cannot be regarded as external products of man's thought and behavior; they are essentially prior to the individual and are indispensable supports of belief and conduct. Release man from the contexts of community and you get not freedom and rights but intolerable aloneness and subjection to demoniac fears and passions. "[20]

The modern social conservative Rick Santorum makes a similar point by balancing the value of rugged individualist entrepreneurs with the need for strong societal foundations rooted in the home. Absent these elements in the increasingly narcissistic and self-centered America of today, the familial model is catastrophically broken.[21] Sadly, the Plural Right is all too often beholden to powerful economic players oriented towards financial profits, and thus sacrifice the family or community without great hesitation. One has only to look at the decades-long ravaging of working class white regions by deregulation and free trade agreements to see how this corrupt scheme progresses; industry departs, drugs replace worship, and insincere Republican politicians promise prosperity to the remaining souls willing to self-improve, cease being a victim, and clean their rooms.

Privilege and Equality

A related consequence of the individual-fixated strand of modern Conservatism lies with its close alignment to the doctrine of equality. Some might regard this as unsurprising, particularly given liberalism's embedding within the Constitution along classical lines of defending individual and economic rights. Of course there are always nuances to the way we interpret said rights, and disagreements about which precisely should be afforded. Conservatives typically embrace negative rights (freedom from), or freedoms to do as one pleases, while modern liberals add on the provision of rights secured through action of the state itself.[22] Proposals like universal healthcare or child nutrition support are elements for this latter advance. Unfortunately, right-wingers often do not know when to stop in pushing for the expansion of freedom, and frequently end up placing individualistic equality over cultural morals. This actually represents a break from the traditions of conservative thought, which hold that a certain privileged, entrenched elite must retain prominence to steer society away from destruction. Friedrich Hayek made a distinction on the matter as follows:

> "A conservative movement, by its very nature, is bound to be a defender of established privilege and to lean on the power of government for the protection of privilege. The essence of the liberal position, however, is the denial of all privilege, if privilege is understood in its proper and original meaning of the state granting and protecting rights to some which are not available on equal terms to others."[23]

Hayek's view on privilege may light the fires of idealism in some hearts, but the tendency of present-day conservatives to concur is actually counterproductive on a societal basis. In their incessant attempt to protect fundamental rights, those on the right-wing actually eradicate the moral primacy of their own elites over national culture. The obvious implication is that a person's behavior cannot be credibly corrected by higher spiritual, social, or political forces. His election for a certain path is bolstered through the inherent virtue that the solitary person knows what is best for themselves and the future.

If the sanctity of the individual is supreme, a complicating byproduct will almost definitely be the provision of rights on an equalitarian basis. The evolution of liberalism creates a reality where no consideration is given as to *who* should possess such rights, or at what age. Placing two teenagers with raging hormones together sans adult supervision could well allow them to fulfill their wildest dreams of sexual liberation, but whether that outcome is desirable remains questionable. If a female becomes pregnant, does liberal individualism permit her to slay the child (violating another's person's rights), or force carrying to term, which might well rustle her own contention of, "my body my choice"? The higher we ascend this tottering ladder of liberal equality the less functional society becomes, until we land at the present, where any and all sick conduct is upheld on an individual basis, although accountability remains quite unheard of.

Equality as a virtue advances to threaten the traditional structures of the nation. Based on the underlying liberal principles backing a fixation on rights, activists will readily seize upon perceived inequalities to indict the authenticity of the system and its supposed commitment to the individual's uplifting. Their ultimate goal is not to simply restore some sense of measured balance and equality, however; instead, they seek to establish a new model where the inequality favors *their* personal or group interests.[24] An excellent demonstration lies with the Black Lives Matter movement, which continued agitating not so much for police reform alone, but in addition, large transfer payments from white elites and corporations to the black community. These included around $50 billion from corporate donors,[25] hundreds of millions in charitable donations,[26] large civil suit settlements with police departments,[27] and the creation of lucrative new jobs catering towards "diversity" interests.[28] In combination, they represent a massive wealth shift which will at minimum empower the rise of a black protester elite with more money and privilege than the working class whites they dismiss as benefiting from innate racial advantages.

America's waltz with the BLM movement provided a further recognition of equality's tendency to change the most fundamental social norms in a parasitic way. The famed sociologist Emile Durkheim established this concept with his "Durkheim constant", an understanding of society in which there must be restrictions on how much deviant behavior can be accepted versus what is seen as normal.[29] If deviancy increases, the social sphere will begin to normalize previously disdainful behavior, expanding its definitions to accommodate the movement. Ideally a balance will be maintained, and yet liberal elites push for increased normalization of deviant activity related to crime, immorality, and degeneracy, while simultaneously attacking traditional behavior as toxic or aberrant.[30] A fantastic example of this would be the assault on law-abiding straight people in favor of gender-bending activists who wish to indoctrinate children into their sick lifestyle. Or better yet, the national deification of George Floyd, a petty criminal and drug abuser, while police officers (symbols of traditional authority) are widely portrayed as sadistic killers obsessed with killing minorities absent cause. The rising criminalization of self-defense is another angle to this dynamic, with Leftist prosecutors trying to imprison or bankrupt those who in past times would have been praised for defending their communities. In the words of Charles Krauthammer, "it is not enough for the deviant to be normalized. The normal must be found to be deviant."[31]

An added problem with the pro-equality position lies in its denial of national preservation through the corrupt ideal of capitalistic meritocracy. Under such terms, economic and educational systems begin skewing towards the global stage, drawing international students and foreign money in some vague, deracinated sprint to the top. Placed alongside offshoring and regional economic contractions, they cast Americans whose lineages goes back to the Founding into a fuming vortex of low wages, debt slavery, and life expectancy decline. Those violated citizens are forced to see culturally and racially alien foreigners rule over them in the championed "civic nationalist" modes of the present day. Any sounded opposition to this crisis is replied to by feathered imbeciles who admonish objectors to, "stop being victims", and "work harder to be better". Of course those retorts are nothing more than shill posturing to defend a moribund global market system that annihilates all sense of kin, faith, and nation. Quite unsurprisingly, the conservative movement is filled with voices endorsing these very destructive ends. The well-regarded neoconservative historian Victor Davis Hanson for instance has openly celebrated the benefits of an American system which affords the same protections, rights, and opportunities equally to fresh arrivals and the descendants of passengers on the Mayflower.[32]

The "Liberal Progressivism is Moral" Paradox

A searing byproduct of the equality principle has been Conservatism's gradual tendency to "follow the leader" when it comes to Leftist ideas about individual emancipation. While right-wing actors will hold the line for a time, they eventually come to terms with the assumed moral supremacy of liberalism and cease taking a firm position to defend social values.[33] Part of the problem here is the Constitution's openness to amendment creation, as well as the activist judiciary, both sowing the potential for expanded conceptions of liberation to become codified and thus difficult to resist politically. Conservative legal beliefs aside, there is nothing stopping the 2nd Amendment from being repealed or modified, assuming adequate support can be found in the House and Senate. Likewise, the Supreme Court can take actions such as the 1973 Roe v. Wade decision on the basis of a particular ideological majority and rule triumphant, even if that position is an anathema to the conservative community. Relativism essentially rules the day, and tacit conservative acceptance of the model actually validates the equal standing of left-wing ideas.

These conditions generate a larger dilemma than most realize. Though modern conservatives usually consider themselves to be Christians with strong opinions on matters like abortion or the family, they stand steadfast in defense of a morally-equivocating structure of laws and governance. Worse still, the consequences of this arrangement are often difficult to rescind. For instance, if a Democratic majority opens the floodgates to non-assimilating immigrants from South Asia, the Middle East, and Africa, conservatives will at best wring their hands over an episode of Fox News, powerless to respond. Never mind that the country's future is being irrevocably transformed against the people's actual wishes; the outcome is ultimately "moral" because the system's design validates it. There is no absolute veto under the written constitution, nor any bridge too far within its legal bounds, and thus nothing can be done until the next election, when civic protections may have already subsumed the undesired populations.

The traditionalist thinker Joseph Comte de Maistre warned of such folly with his discourses against the liberal ideas of the Enlightenment, which he termed, "an insurrection against God."[34] In his view, stooping to the level of erecting a written constitution rejected the foundational premise of God being the true creator of such documents and the giver of laws. Any attempt by humans to assemble supreme legal codes through the state served to diminish the role of the Creator in favor human incompetence, with a more sinister agenda of rejecting original sin and placing destiny in the hands of mortal men.[35]

We see the wisdom of Maistre's arguments in America today. Since conservatives tend to tacitly accept the legitimacy of liberal victories contained within the political exchange model, they gradually come around to whichever positions were at one point exclusive to Leftists alone. Gay rights are a phenomenal example, with Rightists shifting from hostility to general tolerance across a few years, sped up of course by the perceived finality of the 2015 Supreme Court decision. Just as frequently, they audition for liberal approval and acceptance, trying to essentially, "outflank the Left". A grand illustration on this front would be the claim that, "Liberals are the real racists." Countless conservatives have wasted political capital on trying to prove the accuracy of this argument, whether it is by insisting Democrats supported slavery over the objections of conservative Republicans, or embracing criminal justice reform that makes society less safe, merely to prove they have adequate pro-black credentials versus the "racist" Left. Of course these efforts are largely futile, as accusations of racism never come in good faith from a liberal; they are designed to avoid serious debate and lock the target into a

Kafkaesque jester dance wherein admitting guilt leads to derision, but denying is also proof of guilt.

In point, Leftist schemers have gained political and social success by allowing their wing to set the paradigms and agenda of public discussion. Conservatives' need for validation from liberals often leaves them unable to provide new ideas to the populace without resting heavily on the crutch of the enemy's terminology and lingo. Most everything they say is an attempt to mirror or one-up progressive talking points (i.e. "All Lives Matter" or, "The intolerance of the Left"), and subsequently they end up boosting the credibility of the other side. As the political scientist David Green notes, "real intellectual victory is achieved not by transmitting one's language to supporters but by transmitting it to critics."[36] On related terms, Samuel Francis pointed out the following: "Because the mainstream Right craves acceptance by the dominant culture, it also accepts, at least unconsciously, the moral legitimacy of the dominant culture, and of its liberal-Left premises."[37]

IV. The Dual Crisis of Conservative Action

Ahead of our ascension onto the plane of policy misfires, it is necessary to understand precisely how core aspects of the conservative outlook on statecraft actually inhibit victory. There is much gnashing of teeth by everyday members of the Plural Right over the perceived sluggishness of Republican politicians to enact the reforms or cuts which they so fervently desire. Said failures are usually explained away by appealing to a truer, purer Conservatism, when in fact the cause is central to the nature of the ideology itself. The two areas where we witness this most vividly are in the antics of conservative institutionalists, and a related fear of employing state power towards objectives.

1. Protection of Institutions

The retired Senator Jeff Flake opens his literary homage to Barry Goldwater by lamenting that, "Though we conservatives are deeply persuaded that our society is ailing, and know that Conservatism holds the key to national salvation—and feel sure the country agrees with us—we seem unable to demonstrate the practical relevance of Conservative principles to the needs of the day."[38] At first glance, Flake's gloominess might be indistinguishable from any of the other countless appeals to a better politics, which typically suggest that human flaws –- and not the nature of the system entirely—stand in the way of effective democracy. In truth, Flake is getting at a problem birthed by the longtime conservative acceptance that existing institutions, even the ones they personally dislike, must be "conserved" on a neutral basis. Rather than wholeheartedly endorsing the muscular flexibility of government processes, they drift into the pattern of lazy stewardship, leading to Disraeli's aforementioned descriptor: "substituting the fulfillment of the duties of office for the performance of the functions of government." The consequence entails self-described conservatives being able to take power, albeit without the tenacity to achieve major political goals.

A shining example for appreciation came in July 2017, when a last-ditch effort to partially repeal the 2010 Obamacare legislation failed on a 51-49 vote in the U.S. Senate. The result was in large part due to the antics of Republican senators Lisa Murkowski and John McCain, whose dramatic "thumbs down" move ended what had been at the time a seven-year odyssey of conservative brinkmanship. Right-wingers reacted by castigating McCain and his fellows as "RINOS", the happy pejorative attached to any figure seen as insufficiently conservative on the ideological front. Truthfully however, McCain possessed a fairly consistent Rightist voting record, and had himself campaigned *against* Obamacare[39] to stave off a primary challenge from the insurgent J.D. Hayworth in 2010. His vote was less reflective of moderate leanings, and perhaps too his perceived animosity towards President Donald Trump. Instead, it represented a stark illustration of how Conservatism fails at policy while winning at conservation of an institution.

The abovementioned statement may sound baffling, but it actually aligns well with the realities of our subject matter. You see, there is a marked difference between the professed ideological principles of the Plural Right, which often display themselves through near-revolutionary demands for reform, and those practiced by governing actors. Layman Republicans and conservatives clearly viewed the Obamacare program as an anathema which had to be removed in order to restore constitutional government and pare back the administrative state. Their solution thus entailed forcing the process through on a bare majority to ensure ideological victory, regardless of negative perceptions by swaths of the public and Democratic Party. McCain and his ilk on the other hand may well have opposed large parts of Obamacare, yet once the bill was adopted, they elected to *conserve* the institutional process of bipartisanship and the filibuster by not going free range with the vote. Indeed, McCain loudly complained a about a lack of "regular order" related to the repeal process,[40] something he would also lament years earlier in defense of friend and Senate colleague Joe Lieberman.[41]

One could readily retort that Democrats enacted Obamacare without a solitary Republican vote, but the Left has never had firm compunctions about protecting the existing order of things; they happily destroy routines to gain or expand power, recognizing that control and influence matter far more than traditionalistic purity. Perhaps McCain and his associates would have agreed to support a scaled-down repeal bill with Democrat support; the answer ultimately falls to irrelevancy. They protected a governing process, blocking the aspirations of less institutionally-committed Rightists who stood to seize the mandate of genuine authority for their camp. Lest some feel McCain is an outlier, it should be noted that Victor Davis Hanson wrote as recently as 2021 about the dangers of abandoning the filibuster and shifting to a bare majority structure for the United States Senate.[42]

It should come as no surprise that this posture has been long-standing for institutional conservatives. While they did aggressively mount efforts against the New Deal policies of Franklin Roosevelt in the 1930s and 40s, once those social democratic programs went into effect the robust opposition of conservatives melted to extremely moderate reformist levels. Dwight Eisenhower admitted attempts to repeal the New Deal would backfire,[43] and Ronald Reagan expressly opposed cutbacks to Medicare and Social Security, two of the most egregious federal programs from traditional conservative perspectives. Reagan's effort to reduce the latter safety net emerged as an amendment which separated the Social Security fund from general operating spending of the government, taxed social security benefits paid, and gradually increased the retirement age for collection.[44]

These items amounted to moderate reform nibbles at a large federal liability, though Reagan himself claimed Social Security had no bearing on the national deficit.[45] George Bush Senior scarcely dared to challenge established institutions during his term of office, instead embracing a moderate agenda of small budgetary fixes with the Budget Enforcement Act, an agreement that helped contribute to later Clinton-era surpluses, albeit without shrinking the federal behemoth in a significant way.

Hopes were high when George W. Bush won the presidency in 2000 campaigning on a "compassionate conservative" platform to reduce government power and stay out of unpopular foreign conflicts. His domestic agenda entailed a move to centralize education policy in Washington D.C. with the No Child Left Behind Act, and the extremely costly Medicare Part D program, which added $102 billion annually to the federal tab. Bush did manage to enact several tranches of tax cuts in 2001 and 2003, the latter package sneaking through on a bare majority with the vote of then-Vice President Dick Cheney. While tax reductions may seem to be a break with conservative institutionalism, they are in fact well-aligned with its values. We do not after all see genuine attempts to overhaul or throw out the existing, regressive tax code. Instead, conservatives adjust standing rates and deductions while avoiding the difficult spending cuts needed to fulfill their claimed ideological positions. Bush Jr. also vastly expanded federal power over terrorism and citizen surveillance as part of a grand, multi-country War on Terrorism that continues unabated to the present day. Such policies added considerable money to the ledger, boosting America's national debt by at least $4 trillion during his tenure.

Trump's entrance into office revealed other institutional conservative roadblocks beyond the aforementioned Obamacare debacle. After narrowly passing the Tax Cuts and Jobs Act in 2017, a program which cut federal taxes (and consequently revenue) by $1.5 trillion,[46] Republicans followed up with a large Defense spending increase and calls for cuts to Social Security and Medicare. These declarations went nowhere due to internal party opposition and lack of bipartisan interest, but neither factor would have completely staved off the possibility of reductions. Under budget reconciliation, Republicans could have conceivably pushed through cuts – perhaps gleaned from Trump's own budget proposals – and thus curtailed at least some federal spending. But of course the institutionalist leanings prevented such decisive action. Majority Leader Mitch McConnell even backed out of a quite modest plan to cut $60 billion in spending with the excuse that 60 votes would be required.[47] Here of course McConnell was deceiving his audience, as only 51 are necessary to make progress on the trimming front. Slashing spending to various NGOs and organizations that launder money back into the Democratic Party would seem to be a logical path for any incumbent party, but the lull of custom and tradition overrode possibilities for genuine action. Saving the filibuster system was more important to McConnell than actually advancing a path to fiscal conservative stability.

2. Fear of State Power

An immediate consequence of right-wing institutionalist attitudes is the failure to utilize state power, even when administrative credibility is at stake. Run-of-the-mill conservatives may not readily accept this reality, but the truth remains that whoever controls the levers of administration must be prepared to defend them, even when times become difficult. Unwillingness to present a strong front through governance results in a loss of face and legitimacy which gets swiftly exploited by the opposition. Although delegitimizing the Plural Left's actions when they hold a majority is quite reasonable, continuing to be afraid of using the state upon attaining control leads to disastrous results. We see a perfect illustration with the recent Black Lives Matter (BLM) riots.

In May 2020, as America reeled from the economic and medical impact of COVID-19, a video went viral depicting the death of George Floyd while in Minneapolis Police custody. Despite the presence of a global pandemic and previously-enacted lockdowns to confront it, millions took to the streets to protest police conduct and perceived racism in America. Laughably, health experts who had formerly declared anti-lockdown protests "super spreader" events contributing to COVID came up with creative ways to excuse the flurry of disruptive assaults on public order by BLM and associated criminal organizations, with some claiming that, "White supremacy is a lethal public health issue".[48]

Already at this junction conservatives should have realized the obvious: the protests were an aggressive hammer blow pioneered by the Plural Left and its wealthy backers to sow dissent and weaken President Trump in the middle of a contentious election year. Reconciliation was never going to work, no matter how much sympathy Trump expressed to black people both verbally and through his signing of sentencing reform in 2018. The Democratic Party machine was leveling a test to his legitimacy as commander-in-chief along the angle of race, which they knew conservatives would almost certainly buckle at rather than holding firm. But while the right-wing could afford to comfort itself by not appearing imperial and potentially insensitive to blacks, they fell directly into the progressive trap of shrinking from the suit of true power.

All this is not to say that no conservative attempted to evade the inevitable collapse. Many in the movement begged Trump to invoke the Insurrection Act of 1807, a federal law previously employed to restore order during riots over the deaths of Martin Luther King and Rodney King.[49] The president himself was vocal about a desire to protect the sanctity of the state, believing that the protests made the country look weak, and wanted to deploy 10,000 troops in D.C. to quell the violence.[50] He further warned that the rioters would be successful if government officials were timid in their responses and failed to control the streets.[51] According to then-Defense secretary Mark Esper, Trump went as far as asking whether protestors could be shot in the legs,[52] while another claim suggests he wanted them physically beaten.[53]

The aforementioned acts would no doubt be controversial, at the very least threading the libertarian needle of state skepticism which we are so used to seeing from the Plural Right. Nevertheless, they show unhesitant commitment to defending the presidential state and, by extension, the constitutional structure of the nation. Shirking from duty, as hand-tied conservatives do, merely legitimizes the violence and disregard for laws that guerilla activists on the Left employ to weaken their enemies.

So why exactly did Trump fail to act? Simply put, because the same brand of institutional politics discussed earlier refused to cooperate with his objectives. Mark Esper was of course incumbent at the Defense department, where he publicly undermined the president by arguing that protests did not rise to the threshold of the Insurrection Act.[54] Supporting Esper's flank on this matter stood then-Attorney General Bill Barr, who describes the left-wing attack on a federal courthouse in Portland as follows:

> "Every night for months, a mob of hundreds of rioters laid siege to the federal courthouse. What unfolded nightly around the courthouse could not reasonably be called a protest; it was, by any objective measure, an assault on the United States government. The rioters arrived equipped for a fight, armed with powerful slingshots, lasers, sledgehammers, saws, knives, rifles, and explosive devices. Early on, the rioters breached the courthouse and started a fire in the building's atrium. After this, as deputies hunkered down inside the building, they repeatedly set the courthouse on fire. During their assaults, rioters would barricade the front door so deputies couldn't get out and then use crowbars to pry plywood off the windows and throw flammable liquids and commercial-grade fireworks into the building. The rioters would also start fires up against the building and then attack federal officers who attempted to put them out—by pelting them with rocks, frozen water bottles, cans of food, and balloons filled with urine and fecal matter, and physically assaulting them with hand weapons, like hammers and two-by-fours."[55]

By Barr's own admission, Antifa violence was, "domestic terrorism",[56] and the attack on the courthouse itself, "an assault on the United States government", yet he refused to countenance use of the Insurrection Act, trying to punt the issue to municipal authorities and hide behind fears of increased escalation.[57] Alternatively, he followed the classic institutional conservative strategy of trying to out-principle the Left by claiming Trump was blocking their "march through the institutions",[58] and speculating as to how they might react to right-wing activists engaging in similar activities.[59] If the aftermath of January 6th, 2021 is any indication, progressives have few scruples about using the full force of the federal government to harass, arrest, and prosecute individuals guilty of far less than the BLM and AntiFa rioters were in their nationwide actions throughout 2020. It's also fascinating to note that during the latter year, the liberal mayor of Washington, D.C., Muriel Bowser, was calling for more aggressive prosecutions of BLM protestors, only to be rebuffed by Bill Barr-appointed U.S. Attorney Michael Sherwin.[60] Quite inexplicably, Barr would later agree that Americans should not trust corporate and governmental institutions, despite his rugged defense of the latter at the Justice Department.[61]

But while Barr, Esper and Co. may be quintessential in their conservative outlook, the consequences should not act to surprise us. Several past scholars have warned of the dangers inherent to this paralyzed thinking exhibited by the intuitionalist when faced with a serious threat to legitimacy and power. Georges Sorel for example left us with a dynamite summary in his seminal work, *Reflections On Violence*. Here he notes how, "the most decisive factor in social politics is the cowardice of the government",[62] and proceeds to describe almost exactly what we saw from Republican limiters in 2020:[63]

> "One of the things which appears to me to have most astonished the workers during the last few years has been the timidity of the forces of law and order in the presence of a riot: the magistrates who have the right to demand the services of soldiers dare not use their power to the utmost, whilst officers allow themselves to be abused and struck with a patience hitherto unknown in them. It has become more and more evident every day that working-class violence in strikes possesses an extraordinary efficacy: prefects, fearing that they may be obliged to use legal force against insurrectionary violence, bring pressure to bear on employers in order to compel them to give way; the safety of factories is now looked upon as a favour which the prefect can dispense as he pleases [...]"

> "A social policy based on bourgeois cowardice, which consists in always surrendering before the threat of violence, cannot fail to engender the idea that the bourgeoisie is condemned to death and that its disappearance is only a matter of time."

Sorel shows us that ideology cannot ultimately be held above the need for a strong and uncompromising state response when confronted with a direct challenge to legitimacy. Conservatives may think they are winning the long game by preventing some possible left-wing tyrant from retaliating using similar methods in future, but their inaction itself renders Conservatism meaningless. What else will you conserve if not the integrity of the leader's throne, which carries constitutional tradition and social values from hundreds of years past? Like the political theorist Lorenz von Stein once noted, a constitution is, "the expression of the societal order, the existence of society itself. As soon as it is attacked the battle must then be waged outside the constitution and the law, hence decided by the power of weapons."[64]

Stein sounds radical, but his views do not venture outside the reasonable bounds of an executive and leader, who must protect both personal credibility and guarantee the constitutional order, or otherwise risk its decimation by terrorist elements. Carl Schmitt outlined this concept by describing how a leader uses certain critical moments to create the *Ausnahmefall*, or "state of exception", wherein extralegal rules or operations can be put forth to safeguard the state and people.[65] [66] These methods, which may include *Kriegsrecht*, or martial law, are justified because of the state's prerogative to preserve peace, and its confronting of irregular conditions:

> "The endeavor of a normal state consists above all in assuring total peace within the state...To create tranquility, security, and order and thereby establish the normal situation is the prerequisite for legal norms to be valid. Every norm presupposes a normal situation, and no norm can be valid in an entirely abnormal situation. As long as a state is a political entity, this requirement for internal peace compels it in critical situations to decide also upon the domestic enemy."[67]

Achieving said tranquility will ultimately necessitate a fierce executive response, not because conservatives desire "big" government, but given their need to *preserve* the viability of constitutional protections for society at-large. No serious right-wing thinker would look at the resourceful savagery of the Plural Left and come away believing they can somehow be brought over to the light with enough viewings of Victor Davis Hanson and associated rapid-fire fact givers. Their broader goal is to destroy the traditional system, while conservatives seek to protect it. Whosoever elects to employ the full brunt of the exception state will end up writing history, while others collapse by the wayside, weakened and ignored by the holders of power.

We see the validity of this approach in countries where conservative leaders have sadly permitted the triumph of the Plural Left. In the case of Nicaragua, Anastasio

Somoza had the opportunity to put down radicalized activists who threatened the seat of power, but opted for the institutionalist approach, believing their rights to free expression deserved protection.[68] In actuality, Leftists simply used Somoza's partiality towards liberty as an excuse to delegitimize his government, and the consequence was a Marxist takeover in the shape of Daniel Ortega's Sandinistas. Similar dynamics played out during the second term of Chilean president Sebastian Pinera. In 2019, protests erupted ostensibly as a backlash over increased public transportation fares within the Santiago metropolitan area, but Leftists used the economic strife as a fig leaf to undermine Pinera's authority and call for a new constitution entirely. Although Pinera initially took a hard line through his Minister of the Interior, Andrés Chadwick, popular outrage over the latter's aggressive treatment of protestors led to waves of governmental capitulations. Chadwick was removed and later impeached, while Pinera dismissed multiple uniformed personnel tasked with handling the public response. Two years later, the ferocity of liberal activists helped elect radical Leftist Gabriel Boric to the presidency, and progress towards a more progressive constitution replacing Chile's conservative 1988 model was well underway. What started as a cost-of-living protest turned into dangerous political change, all due to a failure by conservative officials to robustly protect the state.

Returning to Trump, his inability to act may indeed be explained by the lack of structural support throughout the Defense and Justice departments, though this intellection relies largely on the assumption that use of the Insurrection Act was his only viable path forward. Anyone with general knowledge of the Constitution will realize that the president need not stoop to the level of employing a mere federal law provided to him like a soup kitchen meal by Congress. Article I, Section IX, Clause II iterates the following: "The Privilege of the Writ of Habeas Corpus shall not be suspended, unless when in Cases of Rebellion or Invasion the public Safety may require it." Nowhere in the same article does it specify a congressional prerogative on the move, and indeed the father of the Republican Party showed us quite ably that a president can act unilaterally. Early in the Civil War, Lincoln suspended habeas corpus to deal with internal malefactors loyal to the Confederacy or opposed to the conflict more generally.[69] Although he faced legal challenges and some legislative opposition, Lincoln was effective at using the tool several times to quell the risk of public chaos generated by the struggle, and left an important legacy rising to our present day.[70] Trump could have employed a similar methodology by simply recognizing the riots for what they were: a violent uprising against the structures of power and the state's legitimacy. Libertarian actors might have attempted to challenge the decision, but his will to act when necessary in those early days could have potentially saved the Republic and his presidency. Ironically, Bill Barr's department requested from Congress extensive emergency detainment powers (without trial) in March 2020, though the policy has not so far advanced to that explicit level.[71]

 Because Trump neglected to act decisively, he was left a shadow of the presidency which his character so long embodied, with masculine energy and disregard for petty feelings as the mainstays. His frequent array of tweets demanding "law and order" whilst criticizing the supposed weakness of Joe Biden on crime fell to scornful ears, for Biden was not yet president and possessed no power to defend the state as Trump did. In fitting fashion, frustration from Trump's followers with seeming administration inaction towards the Plural Left would boil over with the energetic protest on January 6th, 2021. Their actions angered the neoconservative legislator Liz Cheney, who claimed that, "[…] the most conservative of conservative principles is reverence for the rule of law."[72]

V. Markets and Welfare

The modern conservative alignment on market-related issues exists as potentially its greatest crisis of success on the political and social level. Earlier iterations varied between agrarianism and industrial interests, but the Republican Party has always been closely aligned with business advocates, if to varying degrees depending upon region. The eastern wing historically skewed more towards Wall Street comforts given its power base in New York City and New England, while Midwestern representatives under Robert Taft Sr. pushed a libertarian viewpoint designed to block the New Deal and generally keep government out of the private economy. Political realities regarding the popularity of FDR's welfare policies caused the GOP to moderate its broader electoral position as expressed by nominees such as Thomas Dewey and Dwight Eisenhower, while Richard Nixon governed in many respects through the use of Leftist policies like price controls and increased environmental regulation. It was not until the presidency of Ronald Reagan that conservatives had a significant opportunity to deliver on their core, supply-side economic message, though ultimately in a mixed fashion, for the donor class proved difficult to work with on full-throated tax reform.[73]

Since the 1980s, conservatives have struggled to provide an economic vision which can truly align with the interests of broad swaths of Americans, and sustain the family-centric model they often celebrate. There is no doubt that low taxes can be beneficial for the middle and working classes, yet the regimented hostility to government expressed by Republicans often leads to counterproductive ends. A chief example of this would be the largely unchallenged tendency of companies to offshore production beginning in the 1970s and accelerating throughout the next two decades. Conservatives were mostly supportive of the trend, arguing that free trade would result in cheaper goods for the emerging service class of an advanced national economy. More Republicans voted in favor of the 1993 NAFTA agreement than Democrats, helping to seal a process that would cost America an estimated 700,000 manufacturing jobs,[74] while destabilizing the Mexican agricultural economy and causing increased illegal immigration through the southern border.

NAFTA had been pushed using the excuse of free trade, but in fact was designed to liberate companies from the protective regulations that made it harder to exploit cheap labor and outsource jobs. The agreement gave firms leverage to demand cuts in worker pay with the alternative threat of plant shuttering and the exiting of jobs from the country. When it came to the approval of the DR-CAFTA trade agreement in 2005, 202 out of 229 Republican House members voted in favor, along with 43 out of 55 Republican senators, this despite warnings that it would do economic damage on the working class similar to NAFTA.[75] The Central

American advancement was one of 14 different free trade agreements finalized by the Bush Administration before its conclusion in January 2009.

A more ironic development would occur during the Obama Administration, when negotiations concerning the Trans-Pacific Partnership trade deal climaxed, having originally been initiated in 2008. The agreement was designed to further unite regional Asian economies with the United States and encompass around 40 percent of the world's trade.[76] Conservative backing was at various times strong, including the encouragement of Senator Rand Paul[77] and then-Speaker Paul Ryan, who only moderated his view based on the political rise of Donald Trump.[78] Not only did Trump disapprove of the proposed agreement, but he went so far as to renegotiate NAFTA in the form of the USMCA, a superior structure with increased protections for the working class. In point, it requires an eventual wage standard of $16.00 per hour for automobiles manufactured in Mexico, putting the onus on corporations to reduce the labor exploitation of previous times.[79] Establishment Republicans were not pleased with this addition, or over the removal of intellectual copyright protections from some drug manufacturers in the final blueprint. This is because conservatives tend to be sadly unresponsive to the influences of multilateral economics. If stronger guidelines are in place, Mexican workers will have an incentive to remain at home, reducing illegal immigration and hampering companies in the U.S. who desire to shortchange American workers by importing cheap labor competition. From the corporate GOP perspective however, the nation-state does not matter and all policy should serve wealthy actors in America and Mexico.

No one should interpret these findings to suggest that trade deals have zero benefit for the country at-large; on the contrary, they lead to cheaper consumer goods and improved supply chains, but at times we must weigh that relative advantage versus the foundational ethics of conservative thought. Few on the Plural Right would describe themselves as anti-family, or indeed diametrically opposed to class ascension as an American ideal. Nevertheless, policies working to consistently hollow-out the working class without providing adequate rungs for transition into the service sector are almost guaranteed to be disastrous. For years companies demanded a college degree to even be considered for an open position, and yet America has not done much to make higher education accessible on a national basis. A hodgepodge of educational systems predominate, with some assuring cheap in-state tuition for residents, while charging those only miles across the border far higher fees. International students are readily recruited with the same greed incentive as a motivator, denying spots (and ultimately jobs) to regular Americans.

While Rightists do condemn the out-of-control federal student aid program, they have seldom taken action to address the matter on a federal level. Public universities are subsidized by taxpayers, regardless if they attend or not, so it follows from a limited government perspective that tuition should be cut or kept low, not used as an alternative tax to extract wealth from middle and working class Americans. We have yet to see any serious effort by conservatives to impose tuition or fee caps on a federal basis, much less willingness to forgive existing government loans to students. This latter viewpoint is puzzling. Standing against government excess and desiring the growth of families means removing needless burdens from the shoulders of the young, particularly in an era of mass inflation and economic uncertainty. On the flip side, constantly siding with economic elites (even when they are anti-national) and crudely labeling those who fall through the cracks as "losers", hardly advances the long-term conservative cause.

Clearer explanation of the establishment perspective must be included here. Traditional supply-siders hold that the wealthier "job creators" should be targeted with incentive policies like tax cuts and deregulation to encourage hiring or entrepreneurship. Such types are assumed to benefit from deals like NAFTA or usual Republican fiscal handouts because the macro-level statistics will play out in their favor. In point, the NAFTA deal is estimated to have made America $127 billion richer based on its terms of trade expansion.[80] Hence a triumphant conservative or libertarian might swiftly proclaim it a success, albeit on the basis of national economic statistics. When light is turned on more complex micro components however, we begin to see a different picture.

GDP growth itself does not imply a healthy economy upon which the rungs of economic advancement can be safely forged. As an example, while NAFTA may have led to a perceived increase in the financial strength of the United States using purely market-based terms, it did not improve the well-being of the common man. Cheaper goods are desirable, but when they come at the expense of decent jobs with wages capable of supporting a family, the long-term effect is hard to endorse. America has for instance lost an estimated 5 million factory jobs in the past 25 years, with mostly low-wage replacements being created in the service sector.[81] Although the new economy features demand for STEM jobs, corporations have successfully lobbied the government to expand visas from Third World countries, flooding the nation with cheap labor to undercut native citizens. Instead of insisting on reforms to protect American graduates and workers, mainline Rightists have continued pushing for lower taxes or deregulation as the solutions to this significant crisis.

If we take marching orders from the socially conservative side of the movement, economic policies crafted to primarily benefit the elite do not seem to warrant wholesale endorsement. Strong families are more likely to remain intact when benefiting from financial stability and some rudimentary social benefits which stave off the possibility of ruin. We see the opposite with the opioid epidemic, which has ravaged areas that formerly had robust manufacturing sectors supporting the community and providing potential outside of poverty and drug addiction.[82] Not all individuals are cut out to be entrepreneurs, investment bankers, or to write code from a remote location; some are more oriented towards physical jobs within a corporate structure, with adequate benefits and the possibility of a dignified retirement. Abandoning them to serve a strange Darwinian market impulse ought to be seen as antithetical to the conservative realm. Likewise, making provisions for some basic government services capable of helping families with healthcare expenses or education should be considered in their broader role as trustees of the national spirit.

Welfare State

Walking close alongside conservative economic philosophy is a leering indignation at those creatures who utilize government support systems. Conservatives are hardly wrong in raging over such abuses, but on the political front they often misplace greater culprits. Earlier iterations of cash transfer programs on the part of the federal government were certainly plagued with issues. The Aid to Families with Dependent Children (AFDC) established by the Social Security Act in 1935 and subsequent offerings under Lyndon Johnson's Great Society scheme led to corruption and abuse befitting the "welfare queen" image trumpeted by President Reagan in the 1980s. This was because little incentive remained for individuals to work their way out of government handouts by getting a job, attaining education, or ceasing to have unaffordable children. They could simply take and stew in a pool of taxpayer dollars while passing life by.

Matters changed dramatically during the Clinton presidency, however. His agreement with Republicans to enact the 1996 Personal Responsibility and Work Opportunity Act restructured welfare policies in a tremendous way, effectively phasing out the AFDC and allowing states more flexibility in administering federal money. The result was multifaceted, with the notoriously expensive AFDC being reshaped into Temporary Assistance for Needy Families (TANF), a program prohibiting participation by any applicant beyond a lifetime total of 60 months. Work requirements were also added to the mix, and caseloads declined 37 percent between 1995-1998,[83][84] with an overall 55 percent drop between 1995-2000, while certain categories of child poverty also diminished.[85] [86]

These outcomes appear to be positive, but for the mainline conservative movement they remain inadequate. Republicans routinely attacked Barack Obama for supporting more spending on welfare, despite the fact that social insurance rolls declined to historic levels during the 2008-2009 financial crisis.[87] [88] What did increase during that period was food stamp (SNAP) usage,[89] perhaps in part as compensation for the broader decline in availability of direct cash transfer programs. In 2011, Obama actually attempted to cut heating assistance to the poor,[90] and some years later went so far as to endorse the chained CPI reform to Social Security cost of living adjustments, which would have led to savings of as much as $112 billion over ten years.[91] Republicans opposed Obama's broader deficit reduction proposal that included the CPI change, while some in the party refused to believe he ever endorsed it, and the GOP proceeded to attack Obama for "trying to balance this budget on the back of seniors."[92]

By 2018, participation in SNAP programs along with associated spending on those offerings was in considerable decline, with 7 million less taking part than in 2013.[93] Nevertheless, Donald Trump during December 2019 introduced rules further restricting food aid access to those ages 18-49 without dependents to achieve projected long-term savings of $4.2 billion.[94] Amid the ensuing economic decline of the COVID-19 pandemic, welfare rolls fell again, despite their potential advantages in helping those displaced by the lockdowns and vaccine mandates.[95] It was even reported in 2021 that many states were sitting on large stockpiles of unspent TANF funds built up over the previous years,[96] when Americans were struggling with unemployment due to the global health scare.

The takeaway is that traditional conservative alarmism about welfare cheats is somewhat exaggerated. Reforms could be added to SNAP under which no checks are given for children born once already enrolled in the program, but otherwise the system is not this garish reflection of government excess and corruption which many pretend it to be. The occasional shock headline will for instance warn people of welfare dependents claiming $35,000 in government benefits for doing absolutely nothing. Closer examination[97] shows that such awards only go to an extremely narrow segment of the population, and certainly not for life. TANF as we know is the primary direct cash payment program available to those seeking assistance, and it permits a total of five years participation across one's entire lifetime. Only an elaborate false identity ruse capable of overcoming modern ID verification and computer records would allow someone to effectively scam the government rolls indefinitely. At best, some modest adjustments are necessary to eliminate persisting incentives, yet the broader structure is hardly some pariah threatening limited government in the Republic.

There is a further aspect to welfare reform which does not get appropriate consideration. Part of the 1996 package was an aggressive restructuring of child support laws to create better enforcement.[98] [99] Whereas in the past states and localities maintained inconsistent policies regarding pursuit of so-called "deadbeat dads", the new statute required them to take an uncompromising role, cracking down on income for single mothers. Then during the early and mid-2000s there came an upsurge in men online complaining about the family court system, which often foists exorbitant child support requirements designed to preserve a woman's previous quality of life with the man in question. The majority of these men tend to express conservative or libertarian views, with special disdain for welfare mothers, though they do not always bother to connect the dots. Diminished direct cash payments may have decreased overall participation in the rolls, but it directed governments to find supplementary money in private coffers by confiscating assets held by men.

The Failure of Corporate Welfare

Outside of the economic threat to workers posed by the conservative alignment with corporate interests, there is a social one. Supporting the financial whims of multinational behemoths has led over time not to business backing for other aspects of the right-wing agenda, but instead a wholesale barrage against it. Despite being granted countless handouts by conservative politicians in the name of jobs and economic efficiency, corporate actors seize upon the most singularly degenerate positions and happily contribute to the suicide of our moral society. Not the slightest shred of favor is returned, and the culture war shifts deftly to an ever-advancing Leftist side.

To illustrate this reality we must first recognize what a corporation is. No, legal entities doing business across borders are not attune to those under Mussolini's Fascism, which were in fact complex administrative units controlled by the state and shepherded to promote pro-national policies.[100] Instead, our corporations exist as agile, rapidly-transforming juggernauts determined to shore up benefits through cheap labor importation and idealized tax climates, even as they avoid offending the Plural Left's subversive plans for the American family. A prime example here would be the collective reaction to Mike Pence's notorious Religious Freedom Restoration Act of 2015. Pence helped enact the legislation ostensibly to cement protections based on belief, albeit in this case expanding them to the realm of for-profit businesses. The bill was no doubt a response to the famous 2012 case in Colorado where a Christian-run bakery was sued by gays for refusing to make their wedding cake, citing personal religious beliefs. The future vice president had in past described himself as "A Christian, Conservative, and Republican in that order", so his posture was not surprising.

As it turned out, corporations disagreed. The business community launched an aggressive economic assault on Indiana's families, withdrawing investment and jobs. Salesforce canceled corporate requirements for travel to Indiana based on the law, while Angie's List tabled a $40 million dollar plan that would have created

1,000 jobs in the state's capitol.[101] [102] One estimate held that Indiana could lose more than $250 million in the aftermath of the bill's passage,[103] and data concerning Indianapolis specifically suggested a $60 million loss for the city.[104]

We might be tempted to assume Pence was an otherwise vigorous economic socialist, attacking corporate interests and insisting on increases to their tax burdens, all to serve the common man. This would be a lively yet inaccurate casting of effective terms, because the future vice president played footsie with the wealthy classes throughout his term as governor. In 2013, he signed a $1.1 billion dollar tax cut which reduced income taxes by an effective 5 percent. The corporate tax rate was also set on a path of reduction from 6.5 percent to 4.9 percent, with the latter being reached by 2021, when it would clock in as the second-lowest in the country.[105] Pence gave the added benefit of signing legislation which prevented municipal governments from instituting wage requirements beyond those mandated by the federal government, and removed wage protections for state-funded construction projects. In short, he was a dutiful servant delivering corporate benefits and advantages for the managerial class. The Pence story shows us that political goodwill cannot be purchased from self-interested economic actors who serve their own bottom line. Corporations will act as they see fit, seizing the financial incentives but otherwise refusing to align with traditionalist positions which protect culture from the throng of modernity.

And it's not the first time they have done so, either. In the mid-1980s, the Arizona state legislature rejected an attempt by Democrat Governor Bruce Babbitt to enact Martin Luther King Day as a paid holiday. Babbitt responded by creating the holiday through executive fiat, and voter backlash by conservatives in 1987 brought to power Evan Mecham, who swiftly canceled the paid celebration and moved it to Sunday. A campaign was consequently launched to recall Mecham, with the wealthy insurance mogul (and later convicted felon) Ed Buck at the helm. After Mecham was forced out under dubious impeachment charges, the NFL attempted to coerce voters into voting for the holiday's restoration in a series of referenda during 1990, using the specter of canceling the planned 1993 Phoenix Super Bowl as a threat. Voters spurned the big corporation, and their failure to bend the knee led to the NFL following through, pulling back millions of planned investments for the Arizona economy.[106]

A similar development played out in North Carolina after Governor Pat McCrory signed the Public Facilities Privacy & Security Act in 2016. This bill was designed to protect families and children by requiring transgender individuals to utilize bathrooms corresponding to their birth sex. As many supporters argued, it would diminish the risk of someone pretending to be the opposite gender and preying on the young in such facilities. Like with Indiana, the corporate front reacted in characteristic horror, deploying a coordinated campaign to cripple North Carolina's economy as punishment for taking a socially conservative stance.[107] Around $400 million was lost to the state over the short term,[108] with a longer view figure of $3.76 billion projected across a twelve-year period.[109]

McCrory himself was no stranger to protecting the monied classes. During his single term in office state taxes were simplified on a flat basis, and the estate tax completely eliminated. Major reductions in bureaucratic oversight of business were achieved through the Regulatory Reform Act of 2013, and the following year's Energy Modernization Act drastically expanded permits for fracking and energy exploration. These amounted to boondoggles serving big business and wealthy elites, yet they fell short of the collaborative muster which conservatives naively assumed would materialize if they showed dutiful allegiance to the cult of Mammon.

Why? The answer lies in a mistaking of corporations (or the market in general) as being somehow "conservative" in nature. George Grant recognized decades ago that capitalism was not operating independently as some vessel for freedom, but rather had joined itself and become heavily dependent on the state for success.[110] One must only look to the corporate-friendly tax deductions, bailout readiness, and Federal Reserve policy advanced by Rightists to see how this dynamic plays out. Because corporations are dependent on the government, they do not necessarily back conservative politicians for the sake of Conservatism, but rather to gain those aforementioned benefits through the state itself. In this way business actors end up allied with the Left, which outwardly condemns the private sector while working in tandem with executives to achieve common goals.[111] Thus we might see Amazon supporting anti-union stances through Republican legislators while aggressively promoting gay pride to avoid alienating their liberal customers or stepping outside of the entrenched leftism inherent to government bureaucracy.

Coming to terms with such a reality is difficult for most conservatives who grew up being steeped in supply-side economics orthodoxy. Apart from some Old Right critiques, such as Edmund Burke's attack on a society which focuses on self-interest over chivalry,[112] or Russell Kirk's somewhat timid observation that, "A conservative order is not the creation of the free entrepreneur"[113] Conservatism is largely content to marinate in the graces of a model holding private business up as a virtue totem. To go against such assumptions as a political actor is to risk the wrath of a well-funded and defensive donor class.

Doing so has become essential, however. Whether we like to accept the fact of not, subverting the economy to the national and cultural spheres is imperative to safeguard conservative values today and going forward. One cannot expect free actors chasing sales and profit globally to limit their scheming at a national border, or indeed respect the social mores designed to protect youth from degeneracy and debauchery. As Vladimir Lenin famously noted, "Political institutions are a superstructure resting on an economic foundation."[114] It might seem odd to select a communist leader for reference here, but his controversial status makes the case even greater. The Russian Revolution was after all funded by Wall Street actors, and yet this did not result in a total subversion of the Soviet economy, cruel though it was, to the capitalist impulse. Russian communists were able to continue pursuing their ideological goals while largely ignoring the expectations of big business that would otherwise present a stranglehold on the national agenda.

Compare this with the track record of "conservative" Republicans. Corporations are all too willing to cooperate if it means gutting labor protections, slashing taxes, or expanding federal defense contracts. However, the moment matters turn to defending traditional culture and the native population, business executives break out rainbow flags and support invasion by foreigners. Loyalty is irrelevant, as they stand stalwart behind the patriotism of profit, a far more universal idea than the love offered by individual citizens for their nation-state. We therefore cannot expect deference or aid on the issues that matter, and should recognize large companies primarily based on their usefulness in fundraising. Take advantage of the financial provisions to attain power, yet swiftly jettison any illusions of submission to them upon attaining office, when the difficult work of actually conserving culture becomes a priority. In this sense we can observe the wisdom of another world leader who said, "Economy must always be the servant of the nation".[115]

Achieving such a vision necessitates use of the government in a judicious manner to favor the national cause. For example, conservative hostility to taxes must come second to the objective of protecting younger generations. Outright banning of pornography or subversive material would be one way to address the problem, though perhaps financial penalization is more advisable. There is nothing stopping conservatives from instituting a 95 percent tax on gross industry profits derived from adult entertainment, including OnlyFans, or a similar assessment on Hollywood in general. The logic stands that executives are free to push their degenerate entrepreneurship, but disincentives will be in place to severely reduce their potential for wealth-accumulation, perhaps steering some in a more ideal creative direction. This is akin to the path taken by the Plural Right in the 1950s with its strict content standards for movies, which created serious consequences for anti-national filmmakers.[116] Additionally, since degenerate profits made under the current tax system are sinful and ill-gotten, we must perceive them as embodying the *herrenlos* concept, ownerless and abandoned based on origin or process. Transferring these monies to the Treasury for disbursement in service of the nation and people is the just position which denies joy to immoral plutocrats.

Moreover, there is documented polling support for tax increases in some areas by Republican voters, so the proposal is hardly taken within the bounds of political suicide.[117]

Environmental regulation is another angle requiring change. It is easy to dismiss all concerns about pollution as climate change alarmism, yet serious problems do result from continuous development to serve the consumerist instinct, and modern farming practices. Conservatives should emphasize through zoning restrictions the importance of maintaining rural, localism-dedicated communities as opposed to those subdivision and strip mall-concentrated models dominated by HOA busybodies and foreigners. They might also push to open up some of the estimated 27 percent[118] of federally-owned land to small organic farmers who can produce healthier food in a country where numerous medical issues are linked to[119] [120] the unsafe and heavily processed consumables produced by big farms and production plants.

VI. The Social Front

Few categories can better crystallize conservative slouching from cultural defense than the somber track record on gay marriage and abortion restrictions. In the former camp, old guard Rightists exhibited an initially strong position, only to cave steadily throughout the years. During the 1940s and 50s, it was widely accepted that employing homosexual individuals in the federal government, especially for national security posts, was fraught with peril. Some went so far as to describe gays as constituting a Deep State-style, "government within a government", and thus harsh measures were put in place.[121] Subsequently, the 1952 GOP campaign platform included a plank condemning "immorality" and promising reforms to the Washington machine.[122] Dwight Eisenhower subsequently addressed the matter in January 1953 by issuing Executive Order 10450, which implemented security standards for those employed by the federal state, placing homosexual behavior on equal footing with alcoholism, instability, and involvement with communists.[123] The president's move caused the discharge of thousands from federal employment, simultaneously advancing social conservative objectives and the limited government aims of the fiscally-minded crowd.

By 1975, the walls were beginning to crumble. In July of that year, Gerald Ford issued revised guidelines revoking the restrictions on federal employment by gays,[124] and a few years later, Ronald Reagan was actively campaigning *against* a California proposition designed to apply Eisenhower-style rules to the public school system.[125] In 1981, social conservatives moved to block federal funding of organizations promoting a gay lifestyle, but found opposition from their own ranks using arguments based on federalism.[126] The Right finally struck back with the Defense of Marriage Act (DOMA), a 1996 federal law defining marriage as being between a man and a woman, permitting states to not recognize same-sex unions performed in other jurisdictions. The dearth of lawsuits filed against DOMA and active campaigning by gay activists ginned up conservative enthusiasm during the 2004 presidential campaign for a federal marriage amendment that would prevent judicial legislating in favor of same-sex unions against the wishes of individual states. President Bush championed the cause, but it only got so far as a 236-187 House vote in 2006, followed by a 49-48 Senate ballot, far short of the figures required for adoption. Nevertheless, a multitude of states advanced constitutional amendments during the 2005-2006 election cycles, resulting in a high of 31 which had banned gay marriage in some form by 2008.

Cracks continued to show, however. In 2010, *National Review* published a column outlining the "conservative" case for gay marriage.[127] This rode with the endless legal broadside pushed by the Plural Left against traditional unions, which culminated with the Obama Administration's 2011 decision to cease defending DOMA in court on the basis of its Section 3 provisions defining marriage. Conservatives reacted through House Speaker John Boehner by using government funds to continue protecting the law, but to no avail. In 2013, the Supreme Court ruled 5-4 in *United States v. Windsor* that Section 3 violated the Due Process Clause of the Constitution by denying the federal estate tax exemption to the spouse of a deceased lesbian. While this decision was largely the result of Justice Anthony Kennedy's socially liberal leanings, it led to a marked shift in the conservative strategy away from cultural hegemony and towards the face-saving of states' rights. After campaigning hard for years to preserve marriage on a *national* basis, they began trying to promote ostensibly libertarian arguments about the value of self-government and determination. These efforts did not persuade Kennedy, who two years later ruled in *Obergefell v. Hodges* that same-sex marriage rights were guaranteed to gays based on the inherent provision of the 14th Amendment. Chief Justice John Roberts would pen a dissent reflecting the newer conservative position:

> "It is not about whether, in my judgment, the institution of marriage should be changed to include same-sex couples." […] It is instead about whether, in our democratic republic, that decision should rest with the people acting through their elected representatives, or with five lawyers who happen to hold commissions authorizing them to resolve legal disputes under the law."[128]

Roberts' argument about elected officials and state legislatures signals an easy cop-out for those who would have at one time claimed gay marriage is a threat to the entire moral fabric of society, regardless of location in the country. Quite unsurprisingly, in 2018 *National Review* put out a piece calling on the right-wing to respect transgender pronoun preferences,[129] and by 2020 activist Candace Owens was describing the 2015 marriage ruling as an achievement of "civilization".[130] The following year, GOP national Chairwoman Ronna McDaniel openly celebrated Pride Month, while several prominent establishment conservatives pushed gay-friendly rhetoric rather than promoting an end to gay marriage.[131] In July 2022, 47 Republicans joined the Democratic House majority in voting for legislation to codify gay marriage nationally, including relatively conservative figures like Scott Perry and Lee Zeldin.[132] Later in December 2022, final legislation passed the Senate with 12 Republican votes, including erstwhile reliable conservatives such as Joni Ernst and Dan Sullivan. Without their support, the bill enacting federal protections for homosexual unions would never have come into effect.

If we go by the earlier discussion that a liberal decision once made is generally defended by conservatives, it seems unlikely that the court will bring an end to gay marriage. Even if they do so, the ruling will almost certainly follow the pattern of their 2022 abortion decision, which failed to declare termination illegal nationwide, instead leaving it up to the states. Hence traditional culture will not be conserved on a national basis, but rather in small pockets based on the prevailing legislature majority of the time. This may be libertine, yet it is far from a moral position.

Abortion

Abortion carries the matter to more gruesome conclusion. Conservatives adopt a viewpoint on the question typically informed by religious ethics and a fusion of the classically liberal individualism mentioned earlier. There remain more contentious debates among libertarians about the degree to which the fetus can be considered an individual, and at what point, or how much restricting pregnancy termination actually undermines the rights of the mother to have bodily autonomy. Generally speaking, similar concerns are not a tremendous issue for conservatives, with the main struggle being over whether any abortion can be justified due to medical reasons, assault, or incest.

It might be tempting to see abortion as an effective example of cultural victory when compared with other issues governed by the state. After all, the American Right has maintained a fairly uniform fixation since the 1973 Roe v. Wade decision on banning (or at least greatly limiting) terminated pregnancies across multiple states. Federal representatives elected during the Tea Party wave of 2010 invested considerable efforts into defunding Planned Parenthood, the family planning and abortion-offering organization controversial for receiving taxpayer money. As with concurrent attempts to eliminate Obamacare, the efforts continuously failed, though one can concede them as symbolic politics for the conservative cause. Nevertheless, when Roe was finally reversed in 2022, the ruling did not actually achieve what more stringent anti-abortionists would have preferred: a sweeping order declaring fetal personhood and prohibiting the procedure nationwide. America instead received a brutally "conservative" response, here using the general purpose of the term. The 5-4 judicial majority failed to "legislate from the bench" as they often criticized the Left for doing. Their act merely returned the matter to the states, where legislatures have authority to hash matters out as they and voters see fit. According to the majority opinion by Justice Samuel Alito:

> "It is time to heed the Constitution and return the issue of abortion to the people's elected representatives. [...]"The permissibility of abortion, and the limitations, upon it, are to be resolved like most important questions

in our democracy: by citizens trying to persuade one another and then voting."[133]

Conservatives celebrated the decision from the standpoint of their hostility to federal control, but in doing so they revealed an embarrassing lack of appreciation for moral primacy and the national concept. The Supreme Court essentially declared it acceptable for states like California to enact exceedingly liberal laws on abortion, providing other regions can also operate in the opposite direction. This means children will continue being killed in blue states, and conflicts shall arise as to law enforcement cooperation when women attempt to travel across borders for abortion services. This is a remarkable aspect to consider because Alito claimed the Roe and Casey decisions failed to settle the abortion issue, and actually "enflamed debate and deepened division". If anything, the hatred and separation will grow worse as starkly different ethical fiefdoms flourish within close geographical range of each other.

In point, conservative hopes for state-based advancements to favor life through the ruling have thus far backfired miserably. The normally red state of Kansas held a referendum on removing abortion protections from its constitution in August 2022 with over 900,000 people voting and 59 percent rejecting the socially conservative measure. A few months later, voters in several states delivered harsh blows to the pro-life movement. In Montana, a ballot measure that would have mandated care for infants born alive after an attempted abortion was turned back by over 52 percent of those voting. A similar majority felled Republican attempts to introduce a constitutional amendment banning abortion throughout Kentucky, another traditionally conservative state. Perhaps most disheartening however was Michigan, which enacted protections for abortion and contraception in the state constitution with nearly 57 percent of votes, reversing the effects of a strict 1931 law on the matter. Alito believed giving power back to the people was wise, but the result actually damaged human life in a tremendous way.

Social morality cannot effectively be maintained on the basis of libertarian, "do whatever you like providing it doesn't affect me" attitudes by policymakers. If conservatives truly believe in the imperative nature of the traditional family and human life, then they must stand resolutely in defense of both as individuals and through the state. This means legislating in such a manner to prohibit heterodox marital unions and barring the exploitive propaganda trafficked by those in the public education system. It also demands the enactment of statutes which make abortion a severe crime in all states, with repercussions for performing doctors and women who seek termination merely due to convenience, without any medical or moral necessity. Concurrently, appropriate community and state programs should be created to ensure that children given up by parents who are incapable of raising them receive proper care and support in a loving home.

On The Role of Women Freedom vs. Traditionalism

I would be amiss to mention abortion and gay rights without incorporating a better understanding of the conservative approach to the fairer sex. On paper, it would appear that Rightists have maintained their more patriarchal standpoints regarding the social role of women by opposing abortion. At the same time, those individualistic, pro-freedom, pro-market tendencies of the modern Republican Party have reduced said values to a relative husk.

From the outset, we must appreciate how the economic empowerment of women inevitably weakens social mores, particularly in a liberal society. Females have been integrated with the functional system of production in the West for generations, going back to the heavily agrarian period prior to industrialization. While large plantations had slaves to utilize, smaller farmers or ranchers on the frontier would have relied on their wives or daughters to perform manual labor in different capacities as a matter of survival. Concurrently, women in many Indian tribes were responsible for the bulk of the productive tasks (such as planting, fishing, and tanning), excepting war and hunting. Factories in the later era turned to working class women for cheaper labor, and in some cases relied on them to serve as "blackleggers" breaking the strikes enacted by male-dominated trade unions. Importantly however, it was customary in earlier American times for a daughter's earnings to go to her parents, thus limiting overall economic independence.[134]

It would be in post-World War II America that the impact of the female economy bore down relentlessly on the social state. Women had already attained a 24 percent workforce participation rate by 1920, but the war effort opened more opportunities to them based on necessity with countless men being deployed. The trend would continue in the 1950s, when many wives began taking up basic secretarial jobs to supplement their husband's income or provide disposal monies for personal use.[135] University penetration only heightened the dynamic, and women went from 35 percent overall workforce participation in the fifties to 60 percent by the late nineties.[136] Modified legal statutes in the 1970s followed the empowerment trend, removing requirements that restricted the renting of apartments and affording of mortgages to single women or those on birth control.[137]

The takeaway? Women nowadays have less reason to embrace the traditional family role and can extend their time "playing the field" as only the cruder varieties of men were formerly known to do. In addition, the female consumer economy has exploded in recent decades, having reached an estimated $20 trillion of global consumer spending by 2009, with estimates rising to or above $30 trillion in the present day.[138] [139] Women are also believed to influence 85 percent of consumer spending decisions in the United States,[140] and have begun penetrating areas of the economy previously less-dominated by their gender.

These figures matter in the context of a conservative movement which staunchly defends the free market capitalist system, or at least attempts the same with varying degrees of success. The Plural Right is generally skeptical of economic regulations, seeing them as impediments to growth and economic prosperity. But if the economy moves against traditional values, it follows that Rightists will struggle to address the problem of social dysfunction caused by young females refusing to settle down and raise children as they did in the past. Capitalism benefits from the enlarged consumer base made up by women, in addition to the expanded labor pool, which permits companies to reduce the higher wages they might have otherwise granted to men in a single-income household era.[141]

Cracking down on feminine participation in the economy would almost certainly hurt capitalism, yet on the flip side trying to "educate" women about the advantages of settling earlier is a task often falling to deaf ears. Today a young woman with minimal talent (but adequate looks) can develop a massive online following through little more than voyeuristic escapades on YouTube, Instagram, TikTok, or OnlyFans. In such settings they earn top dollar by feeding off of the increasingly disenfranchised young men who previously would have married early and been providing fathers. This contributes to widespread social instability and actually heightens the tension between the genders rather than drawing them closer together, strangle-holding the national birthrate and justifying subversive demands for mass immigration from the Third World.

On the governmental plane, conservative activists has done little to actually hold back the tide of domestic feminism. Under the administration of Ronald Reagan, the progress towards further integration of women in the armed forces only accelerated, with Assistant Secretary of Defense Korb promising a focus on dismantling "any institutional barriers that still exist" within the military.[142] His superior, DoD head Caspar Weinberger, softly opposed allowing women in combat, but did nothing to effectively resist the feminist lobbying campaign, at one point actually suggesting a compromise wherein females would be deployed to the front but then evacuated once hostilities commenced.[143]

The aforementioned push for feminism might explain conservative posturing against actual manifestations of traditionalism in other cultures. Those old enough to remember the christening of America's War on Terror likely recall George W. Bush's fixation on defending the nation against "enemies of freedom" in the form of Muslim terrorists. During his September 20th, 2001 address to Congress, the president mentioned freedom thirteen times, while noting that the terrorists, "hate our freedoms".[144] Because Al-Qaeda and the Taliban subscribe to traditional views on the role of women in society, neoconservative Republicans make the argument that America must stand against the oppression of Muslim women, who are required to wear varying degrees of concealing robes and veils based on the culture where they live. Iran is a particularly strong target for their rage in this regard, as restrictive expectations for women there are contrasted with the freedom fixation of United States culture. To stave off a potential threat from such imported norms, in 2016 a Georgia state representative attempted to expand an existing law on face coverings which originally targeted the KKK, claiming Islamic head coverings could pose a security threat if used as a disguise for criminal activity.[145]

The entire frame of discussion seems undesirable. Though we may dislike the more extreme methods seen in Iran's religious police operations, there can be no question that American women would benefit from a return to cultural norms reflecting feminine modesty and family-centric living. Females being free to have loose sex from a young age has not benefited them whatsoever; it merely leads to the development of emotionally damaged and trustless creatures that are manipulated by short-term men with corrupt intentions. Similarly, working long hours for a corporate bureaucracy as they gradually descend into an embittered misery spiral of therapist visits and antidepressant prescriptions holds no value to feminine advancement. At best these trends make women useful cogs in the neoliberal machine, grinding out a torrid consumerist existence that becomes more soulless by the day. Modesty and tradition will not hurt them, but in fact create better conditions for both genders.

VII. Race and Immigration

A critical challenge for the triumph of Conservatism has been fielded by its response to race and migration issues. Both topics are understandably complex and controversial, often becoming the subject of deflection or denialist tactics by those unwilling to be courageous in their approach to life. Hiding from them does no favors to our pact with truth, however, and thus a steady hand is called for. The objective of prime importance in achieving any headway here is to respect the status of America's nation-state structure along a historical basis, and realize that civic nationalist conceptions are a very new, highly progressive, possibility.

Founding Impulses

We can certainly concede that the majority of the Founding Fathers were opposed to slavery on moral grounds, even if they may have owned slaves themselves.[146] With that said, it would be wrong to weave some fantastical yarn about Conservatism being somehow on the "anti-racist" side of the spectrum. What we in fact see throughout the development of American politics is a dynamic process of variation based on region and political interest. Yet, because honesty does not serve the interests of money-making, conservative talking heads often misrepresent whole swaths of history to benefit themselves.

Let us take a moment to remember what America was actually founded on. A conservative interloper who has recently been trafficking his revisionist books to Fox News claims the Founding Fathers valued diversity as a strength,[147] hence the Constitution's inclusion of the 14th Amendment. Laying aside the fact that the last Founding Father died in 1832, thirty-five years before the amendment came into effect, his view does not even remotely coincide with historical facts of the nation's establishment. Most legal historians are aware of the Three-Fifths Compromise, a component in the Constitution which allowed for the consideration of slaves as not full individuals where population counting and electoral distribution were concerned. More to the point however, George Washington signed the 1790 Naturalization Act in response to petitions pushed by antislavery activists. This legislation, enacted only fourteen years after the Founding and one year into Washington's presidency, restricted naturalization to "free White person(s) of good character", excluding other racial groups and indentured servants.

Washington's law would only become invalidated by the 14th Amendment seventy-eight years later, and under constitutionally dubious terms. Because the former Confederate states refused to endorse the sweeping legal postulate, Congress passed the Reconstruction Acts and imposed military rule over the

South, coercing them into ratifying the new standards. Thus to suggest there is something conservative about the pluralist message, or that it dominated America since 1776, requires one to stretch the fullest bounds of human belief. Indeed, none other than the late Judge Robert Bork observed that the Constitution would likely never have come into existence if America had been a broadly diverse and multi-ethnic nation at the time.[148]

Racial Development and Conservative Revisionism

Much as conservatives decry the possibility of socially engineering a flawless society, they are not free of the idealization streak where American constitutional structures are concerned. It would have been quite stunning to hear a mainline Rightist in the 1950s declare the nation an entirely civic nationalist project without ties to at any ethnic association. Nevertheless, after demographics changed rapidly during the 1990s and 2000s, it became common for less ancient figures to make precisely this argument. Conservatism once again adapted to changing times, specifically by rewriting historical norms to promote an ostensibly pro-diversity message. They were greatly aided here by the likes of gatecrashers such as Dinesh D'Souza, a tremendously successful charlatan who manages to soothe the bothered nerves of those white conservatives accused of racism by reinventing American history entirely. Under D'Souza's model (no doubt partly self-serving given his ethnic origins), the American Right was always a bountiful flagon of activism promoting individualism and racial pluralism, while lefty-liberal Democrats conspired to keep people of color generally (and blacks specifically) socialized under the manacles of slavery. Problematic for such a narrative is its inherent historical contradiction.

While we can agree that Abraham Lincoln was a Republican who took action against the South that ultimately freed the slaves, he did so by violating every basic precept of limited government through his invasion of the secession-favoring Confederate States of America (CSA). Lincoln suspended habeas corpus and used federal troops in a costly war that completely upended the federalist principle and took a sledgehammer to belief in state sovereignty. The succeeding Republican Congress then passed laws denying Southern states self-government until they ratified the 14th Amendment, which was broadly opposed in the region.

In contrast to Lincoln's aggressive use of executive power, the South adopted a constitutional structure which in various ways sought to conserve liberty by delimiting tyrannical behavior on the part of the central government. Even a cursory look at the CSA's constitution demonstrates it to be far and above the popular reformist dreams of conservatives today. To start, the document enshrined the principle of a legislative veto, which permits the president to selectively remove certain appropriations (spending) that he deems unnecessary rather than rejecting the bill wholesale. Any conservative worth his weight in salt will constantly rant about the need for such a provision in America today, and yet the Supreme Court almost unanimously invalidated an act seeking to do just that in 1998. The Administration of George W. Bush attempted to revive a weakened version of the legislative veto in 2006, but it went nowhere in the face of unified political opposition. One can only imagine how much spending might not be on the books if the president possessed such power.

Confederate legal theorists included several other key conservative reforms in their overarching document. For one, bills were mandated to be simple, narrow in scope, and clearly account for all expenditures with public transparency. Congress could only enact a spending bill with a two-thirds vote in the affirmative, and any attempt to raise taxes demanded the very same number in support. Fused together, these first principals embody the bulk of the 2009 Tea Party movement's fierce revolt against a government perceived to be too large, oppressive, and greedy. To crown these restrictive reforms, the authors of the CSA constitution locked the presidency into a single, six-year term of office, with candidates being chosen by the states in a collective fashion. The process for establishment of a constitutional convention was further simplified, allowing state governments to rapidly advance potential constitutional amendments that might protect their rights or hold back corrupt manifestations of power by federal officials. Again, the hand-wringing of conservatives in modern times could have well been addressed by a CSA-adjacent model of state administration, but its mere association with slavery makes the typical Rightist hold back in pronounced horror.

Modern conservatives usually justify Lincoln's actions by arguing he had no other choice in protecting the individual rights of enslaved Africans living within the United States.[149] Such a position is simply not logical when put up against scrutiny. The British Empire managed to end its system of slavery in a largely peaceful manner, by purchasing the freedom of individual slaves and gradually attaining liberation without a destructive war. It should also be noted that the Confederacy had already begun the process of winding down the trade by constitutionally prohibiting the importation of further slaves, though slavery itself was not abolished. Remarkably, Lincoln's edict freeing slaves in the South did not apply to states in the North, where he had direct authority, thus ensuring less immediate economic disruption for his side as the conflict raged on. He was also sluggish to expand protective rights for black people in the judicial system, despite his image as a civil rights president. Dinesh D'Souza weakly excuses these behaviors in his *Death of A Nation* book by claiming the president was playing politics with Union Democrats to advance incremental change, and protecting a program of consent by the governed.[150] Later on in the same text, D'Souza condemns FDR for making deals with Southern Democrats to advance elements of the New Deal, even though these programs did provide some basic help to blacks.[151]

Other areas of D'Souza's book make grand attempts to muddy the waters of historical understanding and reinvent conservative history. He for instance tries to discredit members of the Alt-Right like Jason Kessler and Richard Spencer for associating with the Democratic Party,[152] as though this affiliation in of itself conveys specific ideology. A similar approach is employed to dismiss both Chief Justice Roger Taney, who wrote the majority Dred Scott decision, by describing him as, "an Andrew Jackson protégé and lifelong Democrat",[153] and President Jackson himself, as a slave owner.[154] What D'Souza conveniently refuses to mention is that presidents Ronald Reagan and Donald Trump were former Democrats, the latter proudly bringing Jackson's portrait into the Oval Office upon reaching the presidency.[155] By D'Souza's logic, Reagan and Trump are forever tarred by their association with the Democratic Party and its legacy of slavery.

Not to be limited, still more material is devoted to gaslighting gullible conservatives into delusional positions. D'Souza claims for example that the "racist" Northern Europe-favoring 1924 Immigration Act was enacted by progressive Democrats and Leftist, "RINO" Republicans, but presumably opposed by "conservative" members in the GOP.[156] A quick check of the congressional record shows that Republicans overwhelmingly favored the legislation, including liberal senators like Henry Cabot Lodge, himself sympathetic to the rights of blacks, and future vice president Charles Curtis, a member of the Kaw Nation. The final bill was signed by President Calvin Coolidge, an arch-conservative and idol of Ronald Reagan who remarked about the legislation, "America must stay American."[157] If we follow D'Souza's mental gymnastics, all of these figures were in fact progressive racists protecting white supremacy, and hence they must be remanded to the hated column of the Democratic Party.

New Deal Clarification

Not only are conservatives supporters of diversity migration in the mind of the revisionist; they also had to stand by and watch as progressive (racist) Democrats laid waste to a limited government agenda by enacting the New Deal. Here again, history should serve as our guidestone in pursuit of the truth. While there can be no question that Republicans were initially united against the social democracy expansion proposed by Franklin Roosevelt, we would be fools to assume complications end there. In 1937, FDR proposed legislation meant to reduce the power of political parties and strengthen the Executive's ability to act independently of the legislature. His efforts were defeated not simply by dissenting Republican votes, but also due to large-scale defections on the part of conservative Southern Democrats, who were concerned over its consolidation of power at the federal level.[158] In response, Roosevelt launched a large scale effort in the 1938 Democratic primaries to "purge" conservative Democrats from the party.[159]

FDR only achieved limited success, as evidenced by the fact that traditional Democrats were aligning with Dwight Eisenhower during the 1950s to defeat liberal proposals like federal education aid for school construction and teacher salaries, boosts to the minimum wage, along with healthcare serving the elderly and poor.[160] It was not until the late 1950s, after liberals began making deeper inroads into the South, that the emerging center-left started dominating the party's representative total.[161] The shift only accelerated after passage of the 1965 Voting Rights Act, and the presidency of Ronald Reagan. During the 75th Congress under FDR, Democrats controlled 117 out of 120 representative seats allocated to thirteen southern states, including all former members of the Confederacy. By the end of Reagan's presidency the total number of seats had risen to 124, but Democratic control fell to 85, and would continue dropping throughout the 1990s and 2000s.[162]

Southern Strategy Reinvention

As history touches the 1950s and 60s, conservatives rely on lamentable arguments to prevail with assumptions about the racial orientation of the two major parties. Their overarching theme suggests Republicans were the party most giddy for civil rights reforms, while racist Democrats merely switched tunes in order to create a reliable plantation of black voters. The reality is somewhat less endearing to the GOP, at least from the standpoint of a modern propagandist. As the Republican nominee in 1944 and 1948, Thomas Dewey pushed for precious little on the civil rights front, for doing so could have proven electorally dangerous as he challenged the might of the Democratic Party, which at this point still had strong dominance in the South. Throughout the presidency of Dwight Eisenhower, a moderate conservative, minimal deliberate action was in fact taken to further the cause of integration. Eisenhower did complete the process of desegregating the military started by Democrat Harry Truman,[163] but expressed dismay over his choice of Earl Warren as chief justice after Warren ruled for school desegregation in 1954.[164] Nor was Ike an equivocator on the matter, advocating instead a voluntarist and localist approach:[165]

> "[...] it is my belief that improvement in race relations is one of those things that will be healthy and sound only if it starts locally. I do not believe that prejudices, even palpably unjustified prejudices, will succumb to compulsion."

The president eventually deployed federal troops to help control violence around the planned integration of schools in Arkansas, but did so reluctantly on the basis of perceived constitutional duty, not personal desire to disrupt a local issue.[166] This was in keeping with the *National Review*, which published an editorial in 1957 aligning with Southern efforts to protect states' rights, only to flip some decades later and cast Martin Luther King as a conservative figure.[167] Furthermore, traditional conservative Richard Weaver defended the South's political administration at the time as a bastion of "independent, self-directing social order" resisting modern subversion.[168] Eisenhower would ultimately adopt an outlook later championed by Barry Goldwater, the noted conservative and GOP nominee in 1964. Goldwater famously opposed that year's Civil Rights Act on the basis of constitutional reasoning, with concurrence from Ronald Reagan himself.[169] Present-day Rightists try to portray the legislation as being a just conservative measure[170] despite its brazen trampling over economic freedoms and the principle of federated administration. The neoconservative journalist Jonah Goldberg goes so far as to describe Goldwater's vote against the behemoth legislation as a mistake which he apologized for[171], while Dinesh D'Souza makes a similar conclusion.[172] These are rather strange contentions given Goldwater's continued defense of the choice in his autobiography, where he explains how parts of the legislation had "no constitutional basis for the exercise of Federal regulatory authority" over matters of employment and public accommodations.[173] As he noted on the Senate floor:

> "I am unalterably opposed to discrimination of any sort. I believe that, though the problem is fundamentally one of the heart, some law can help; but not law that embodies features like these, provisions which fly in the face of the Constitution."[174]

Goldwater's position is amiably proffered by a constitutional conservative point of view, where the supreme document remains: "a system of restraints against the natural tendency of government to expand in the direction of absolutism."[175] It pales however against the desire of modern conservatives to protect what is now an established institutional order created by their liberal counterparts with the civil rights and administrative state. They move in patterns attune to the present political pulse, "re-expressing their convictions to fit the times"[176] by imagining the American Nation in creative and ahistorical ways. Thus, despite the hostility of the Founding Fathers to pluralism and their restriction of the vote outside a limited, white, land-owning elite, the conservative saga confidently co-opts these later enfranchisements as if they existed since time immemorial.

Recent Conservative Spin

Against these realities, modern conservatives persist with their revisionist arguments. Victor Davis Hanson for instance argues that civil rights legislation made race irrelevant under a creedal system of meritocratic citizenship.[177] He readily quotes Teddy Roosevelt to argue in this fashion,[178] perhaps forgetting the 25th President's unflattering views of non-European groups:[179]

> "The most righteous of all wars is a war with savages, though it is apt to be also the most terrible and inhuman [...] A sad and evil feature of such warfare is that whites, the representatives of civilization, speedily sink almost to the level of their barbarous foes."

> "I know what a good side there was to slavery, but I know also what a hideous side there was to it, and this was the important side."

> "I do not believe that the average Negro in the United States is as yet in any way fit to take care of himself and others as the average white man, for if he were there would be no Negro problem."

The takeaway according to Hanson is that America must strive to educate a vibrant class of civic-minded individuals who are committed to the ideals of the Republic and conscious of their own role in preserving it. Earlier immigration laws favoring Europeans are discriminatory from his perspective, so the country should avoid retrenching into nationalistic or tribalistic positions, focusing instead on multiracial unity.[180] At the same time, he admits that the overwhelming tide of migration from Asia, Africa, and Central America is rapidly changing America by not affording enough opportunities for assimilation and intermarriage.[181]

Nothing better may explain the crisis of conservative thought in this regard. America needs a population reverent of the Founding Fathers and constitutional principles, but said objectives must be achieved in a non-exclusionary manner. Hence we are supposed to believe that blacks collectively and those originating in countries impacted by colonialism will simply find their way to admiring rich, white landowners based on the Enlightenment values enshrined within the Constitution. While there are no doubt some swaths of the country capable of attaining such understanding through civic education, it is flagrantly unrealistic on a large scale due to history and the advantages of opposition narratives in public schools. No amount of shrill appeals to "teach" minorities, as conservatives often suggest, will surpass these factors, and certainly not in time to preserve the country.

Even if Hanson's vision were realistic, it relies on a rose-tinted assumption about America birthed in the majority-white era of the 1950s and 60s, when he was a young man. It is not the case that race was set to become insignificant before the rise of a politician such as Obama, like Hanson suggests; in reality, the demographic position of whites—and especially white men—nullified any real possibility of an electoral threat from other populations. Minorities were left to either assimilate into the mainstream fold or adopt an independent identity that would be ignored (or suppressed) based on the specific context. As populations shifted noticeably in the 1990s and 2000s, with the white share of the electorate steadily dropping,[182] formerly ignored racial identities gradually gained public currency, opening a path for Obama's triumph. For few other reasons might we witness the Republican Party progress from vetoing civil rights legislation under Ronald Reagan[183] to wasting political capital in enacting the First Step Act, a sentencing reform bill designed to gain black votes. Or more egregiously, President Trump's embarrassing, $500 billion Platinum Plan welfare proposal, which was fashioned to expand federal hate crime charges and establish the Juneteenth holiday. More recently, conservatives have taken a stand against Critical Race Theory being taught in public schools, usually promoting a colorblind message versus the identity politics of Marxist teachers.

Not only do conservatives adapt politically to keep pace with the Left; they also attempt to out-diversify their opponents in a questionable manner. After Mitt Romney was condemned for saying immigrants would "self-deport" during the 2012 election cycle, the Republican Party became increasingly paranoid about racial perceptions, compiling an entire report supporting inclusion and addressing desires for, "a more welcoming form of conservatism".[184] Even before this moment, conservatives revealed a striking obsession with being pantomimes for their opponents on questions of racial politics. Their first move was to elect an RNC chair with no particular qualifications or success at fundraising in the shape of Michael Steele, the former lieutenant governor of Maryland. The decision to anoint Steele was described years later with brutal honesty by staffer Ian Walters at the American Conservative Union:

> "We were somewhat lost as a group, [...] We had just elected the first African-American president and that was a big deal. And that was a hill that we got over, and it was something that we were all proud of. And we weren't sure what to do. And a little bit of cynicism, what did we do? This is a terrible thing. We elected Mike Steele to be the RNC chair because he's a black guy, that was the wrong thing to do."[185]

Walters was dragged for his comments, yet they speak to a significant reality surrounding the antics of conservatives in the modern era. Desperate to fulfill the publicly-declared expectations of "anti-racist" liberals, they look for any tool of deflection to one-up the opposition force. In point, the same year Steele left office as RNC chair, conservatives temporarily rallied around the presidential campaign of pizza executive Herman Cain, an affable individual with horrendous understanding of economic policy and foreign affairs. Cain was however African-American, giving him an attractive selling point for those conservatives exasperated over being labeled as racists by the Democratic Party machine. His moment in the Republican spotlight would subside quickly due to multiple accusations of sexual harassment, and even fellow travelers like Allen West or Ben Carson have been short blips on the political radar.

During the Trump years, increasingly slavish conservative apologetics over race were laid bare. A viral video published by the former liberal Candace Owens quickly garnered her mass popularity as an aggressive minority advocate for the Republican Party. That Owens herself had a well-established history of playing the race card for personal benefit and trying to eliminate privacy protections on the internet mattered not; she was an effective voice for Conservatism and physically attractive versus the stereotyped ugly women of the Left. She also provided conservatives tired of race-baiting with an ideal shield against the opposition narratives regarding their "true" feelings towards blacks. The most notable use of this tactic was her creation of the Blexit movement, a supposed large-scale exodus of blacks from the Democratic Party and its "racist" plantation policies to supporting the apparently multiracial and tolerant GOP. Donald Trump lent credence to the cause by visiting a black conservative summit in 2019, and went on to propose the aforementioned $500 billion socialist giveaway supporting African-Americans before the 2020 election.

What emerges from the aforementioned approach to race is a fundamentally paternalistic attitude by conservatives towards the black population. While the Plural Left plays a maternal role, promising to rescue blacks from racism and give them more government funding, conservatives act as if the historically enslaved population cannot think for itself and must be rescued from Democratic Party brainwashing. Astute political observers may pick up on the broader theme by considering how alignment with blacks is treated like a divine and moralistic symbol in American discourse, a "Mandate of Tyrone", if you will. Democrats for instance latch onto the death of George Floyd to showcase their claimed commitment to protecting minorities from police overreach. Republicans respond by arguing they wish to free blacks from the Democratic plantation and save black babies from abortion. As a clear example, we have the likes of Bill Donohue, a strong Catholic and conservative who reacted to black female politicians endorsing abortion after the Roe v. Wade reversal as follows:

"White supremacists have always championed population control for blacks, whether it be in the form of birth control or abortion," [...] Today this cause is being led by black Congresswomen. [...] Rep. Pressley is not only ignorant of history — she has become an existential threat to the health and safety of African Americans. [...] How ironic that she is now on the same side as the Klan."[186]

Beyond Donohue's grousing over white supremacy, a rather clownish term with no real meaning outside liberal circles, he proceeds to inject himself (and white conservatives more broadly) into a community as moral saviors of the people. Blacks effectively cannot be trusted to make decisions or elect their own leaders under this popular conservative perspective. They require rescue by the shining horse of the pro-life activist, who will constantly preface his statement in opposition to abortion by noting how 40 percent are done to black babies. Doing so gives him ethical cover to criticize the "baby killing" liberals while casting them as horrid racists who hate African-Americans in general.[187]

The irony of course is that the supposed pro-multiracial, "judge by the content of their character" bent of the GOP is merely an idealistic veneer to place overtop obvious ethnic politics. As we saw in earlier paragraphs, Republicans were not so much trying to fashion their message to appeal universally, but rather trot out figures who might curry favor with specific racial constituencies. The idea behind Steele, West, Carson, and Cain is not simply philosophical inclusion, but a signaling to black people that others who look like them support Conservatism, suggesting the possibility of racial solidarity around that position.

The 2021 statewide elections in Virginia proved this point admirably. Republicans opted to run a white, moderate-seeming financial executive in the form of Glenn Youngkin who leaned into the culture war by promising to ban Critical Race Theory in public schools. Here we have an ostensibly colorblind position, as CRT opponents often cite Martin Luther King on content of character to dispel Marxist teachings on race. While that may be a reasonable strategy, the GOP proceeded to nominate a Hispanic (Jason Miyares) for the attorney general race and a Jamaican woman (Winsome Sears) to serve as lieutenant governor. In other words, they produced a ticket not fixated merely on content of character, which can be exhibited by any race, but in fact specifically targeting various racial groups with appeals to diversity and ethnic inclusion. Interestingly, Sears had previously launched a Senate write-in campaign to protest as "racist" the GOP candidacy of Corey Stewart, who evoked a more explicitly pro-white position than she appreciated.[188] Hence ethnic appeals are acceptable for conservatives, especially if directed towards blacks, Hispanics, Asians, or Jews, but in the case of whites, the comfort level declines dramatically. To illustrate the extent of the dynamic,

Youngkin would go on to appoint a chief diversity and inclusion officer after his in inauguration in 2022,[189] while Miyares established an anti-Semitism taskforce the next year.[190]

Whether all these efforts to shill actually work is certainly debatable. Republicans won in the 2021 race, albeit narrowly, with the largest margin going to Youngkin (64,000 votes), about 50,000 for Sears, and barely 27,000 for Miyares. The race took place only a year after Trump's performance in the presidential election, when he pulled a weak 12 percent of the black vote and 32 percent of Hispanics,[191] less than the 44 percent of Latinos secured by George W. Bush in 2004. Statewide elections in Georgia in 2022 provide an even clearer picture of the payoff. Republicans put great effort into securing the nomination for Herschel Walker, a retired football star and fitness advocate of African ancestry. Placed up against incumbent Democratic Senator Raphael Warnock, also black, Walker won a measly 8 percent of his demographic's vote and lost the election. In comparison, Republican Brian Kemp (white) ran for reelection as governor in the same month and defeated Stacy Abrams, who is black, in this case taking a marginally higher percentage of the African-American vote. What Georgia shows is that simply putting up a diverse candidate will not persuade voters that conservatives are "non-racist", or somehow deserving of equal footing with the progressive front.

Conservatives would likely perform better if they stuck with a message guided by the interests of the country's heritage founding stock. Obviously non-whites will participate, but it must be on the basis of genuine conviction and belief, not following the dictates of a desperate party attempting to deflect nasty slurs from the Left. The personal transformation remains critical because changing economic conditions alone are not adequate to shift ideological loyalties. One might assume the growing black middle class will be naturally Republican, and yet outreach has failed to translate into votes because conceptions of racial self-interest are so incredibly powerful. Judge Robert Bork outlined the issue with his discussion of "race holding", a concept wherein blacks who have gained economic advantages (even over many whites) will continue playing the race victim card because it is a valuable tool to get ahead in society.[192] One can claim racism and be considered for a promotion or attain access to the elite by shaming the existing order into feeling guilty for past conditions. All these realities imply the "natural" conservatives who come from the black community will be those deliberately rejecting the politics of manipulation, and likely arrive there based on their own intellectual endeavors, not in response to Fox News talking heads.

Immigration

Race may be the larger issue, but its ties to immigration are undoubtedly in need of separate consideration. Since at least the 1700s, migration to America has created a winsome matter in the realm of politics, managing to capture various factions or ethnic groups in a conflict with others. Benjamin Franklin railed against perceived shortcomings in the German-American population, urging that their numbers be restricted. Italians, Irish, Slavs, and Chinese all faced varying degrees of hostility as they arrived in significant numbers, shifting electoral alliances and impacting emerging economic dynamics in the nation.

In the 1920s, a backlash which had been brewing for some time resulted in more restrictive migration laws. Although commonly described as the byproduct of aspirational racialists like Madison Grant, these pieces of legislation were in fact designed with more nuance than the typical spectator realizes. Organized labor had long been complaining about the heavy waves of immigration from China on the one hand, but also Southern and Eastern Europe, which sourced hundreds of thousands relocated to overcrowded American cities. Impoverished survivors of the First World War also attempted to gain access to the United States, furthering the problem's visibility. These migrants were a plentiful boon to large corporate interests, which sought cheap manpower to drive down costs and improve overall profits. Furthermore, black American leaders supported immigration restrictions, fearing that inexpensive European workers would undermine the ability of their own people to gain stable employment.[193] Hence the 1921 and 1924 acts were not crafted primarily with the intent of excluding non-whites, as modern progressives suggest; rather, they sought to boost wages and stop the population concentrations in urban regions, which struggled with sanitation and housing issues. In final terms, the group most distinctly affected was Italians, who declined from a nationality cap of almost 12 percent or 42,057 people to 2.34 percent or 3,854 people between 1922-1924, and had only recovered to 3.57 percent by 1925. Several Slavic nations saw drastic declines during the period as well, revealing the actual orientation of the legislation as being against certain European groups.

Nevertheless, the 1924 legislation did not fail to provide corporations with a consolation prize for their loss of cheap European labor. Notably exempted from the national origin caps were countries in Latin America, which became the focus of private sector recruiters after Italian and Slavic options dried up. As evidence of this we have immigration data for the period of 1910-1940, when Latin American migrants accounted for 30 percent of those entering the United States.[194] Hispanics even became beneficiaries of the special *Bracero* program starting in 1942, which allowed them to serve as guest workers for the agricultural industry, with tens of thousands taking part before its termination in 1964. So in reality, Hispanics were favored over many Europeans at least until the aggressive liberal reforms of the mid-1960s.

Successive laws in 1952 somewhat relaxed the conditions imposed by the 1924 bill, but maintained a firmly North and Central Eurocentric concentration for migrant origins, while still permitting substantial immigration from the Hispanic realm. It would take another thirteen years before the issue was revisited with the Hart-Celler Immigration and Naturalization Act of 1965. This new legislation was enacted due in large part to the heavy Democratic majority in both houses of Congress, which now had more liberals and moderates in the caucus than conservative Southerners.[195] Hart-Celler was advanced in rejection of prior attitudes seen as restrictive towards not just Catholics and Slavs, but also the Jewish refugee population, which was not readily accepted into the United States during the period of Nazi dominance in Germany.[196] Quite fittingly, the two prime sponsors of the legislation were Senator Ted Kennedy of Massachusetts (Irish Catholic) and Representative Manny Celler of New York (Jewish). Both framers achieved the bulk of their goals by eradicating the older nationality caps in favor of broad-based regional allowances which rested parts of the world outside of Europe and Latin America on equal footing with the traditional heritage centers. Senator Spessard Holland, a conservative Democrat from Florida, lamented at the time: "Why for the first time are the emerging nations of Africa to be placed on the same basis as are our mother countries, Britain, Germany, the Scandinavian nations, France, and other nations from which most Americans have come?"[197]

Pushing back on conservative objections, Manny Celler promised the bill would result in an insignificant amount of immigration to the United States, while Kennedy noted that: "This bill will not flood our cities with immigrants. It will not upset the ethnic mix of our society."[198] To assuage some of the less persuaded in their party, the two legislators agreed to a compromise wherein a 120,000 entry cap would be placed on the Western Hemisphere (versus 170k for the Eastern Hemisphere), effectively suppressing migration numbers from Latin America and the Caribbean in exchange for the massive surges brought on by the liberalization of Asia and Africa.[199] Chain migration furthered these latter shifts by allowing individuals to sponsor large numbers of adult relatives through the mechanism of family unification. The policy translated into a dynamic where immigrants brought in and naturalized as part of the initial chain could turn around and sponsor those close to them,[200] creating an almost limitless stream of new entrants. Although the law officially capped entries at 290,000 annually with 20,000 per country, family unification ballooned it far beyond that level.[201] Results of these more loose provisions can be seen in the regional shifts of migration origin during the decades after the bill's passage, with Europe and Canada dropping from 45.9 percent to 17.1 percent, Latin America and the Caribbean increasing from 39 to 47.2 percent, Asia jumping from 13.4-30.7 percent, and Africa more than doubling from 1.8 to 5 percent.[202]

While Hart-Celler was bad enough, it was followed by two pieces of legislation meant to expand the radical demographic displacement of European-Americans in the United States. The initial salvo came about under the presidency of Ronald Reagan and was named the Immigration Reform and Control Act of 1986 (IRCA). Here materialized a law designed to effectively solve the illegal immigration issue by instating penalties on employers and more robust enforcement in exchange for a large-scale amnesty of 2.7 million illegal aliens. Reagan remarked on the bill's passage that, "future generations of Americans will be thankful for our efforts to humanely regain control of our borders."[203]

In theory, the optimism expressed by Reagan held promise. After all, the IRCA had moved to aggressively target employers who hired illegal workers with civil and criminal sanctions by instituting stricter checks and a fraud-proof work authorization system. In reality, fraud was rampant, and an electronic verification model such as E-Verify has never been adopted nationally without exception. An added issue was Reagan's conservative attitude towards big business, which resulted in his immigration appointees watering down the enforcement angle to allow for lower fines than the law initially established.[204]

George H.W. Bush entered office in 1989 and continued the disastrous policies of Ronald Reagan on migration, refusing to aggressively police corporate malfeasance towards the law and American workers. His more prominent achievement however was the Immigration Act of 1990, a horrendous piece of legislation that served to barnstorm the floodgates of legal immigration by drastically increasing the number of visas issued each year. Despite making some modest reforms to tighten family unification eligibility, the bill expanded unification allowances overall, and increased total immigration to a 700,000 limit, while boosting visas by 40 percent.[205] The 1990 legislation also moved to introduce a "Diversity Lottery" program, created the Temporary Protective Status system, eliminated English testing requirements for longtime permanent residents, and removed a ban on entry by homosexuals. Today, over 1 million legal migrants enter the country annually, around 2 million gain access through temporary visas (which they may overstay on),[206] and millions more may enter through illegal means.[207]

Not all proved gloomy, however. Conservatives did win some minor victories during the 1996 sessions, passing two anti-immigration bills and the famous welfare reform legislation. The Antiterrorism and Effective Death Penalty Act (AEDPA) started off these improvements by simplifying the process for removing criminal aliens from the country, along with those who commit terrorist offenses. It would later be built upon by the REAL ID Act during the 2000s, a useful tool for future removal efforts. Also in 1996, the Illegal Immigration Reform and

Immigrant Responsibility Act (IIRIRA) created much harsher entry bans which would deny repeat offenders visas and expand the definition of aggravated felonies, while further banning non-citizens from voting. The welfare reform bill instituted during that same year barred illegals from utilizing social benefits and put a five-year waiting period on qualified immigrants seeking federal public benefits.

Besides the REAL ID legislation of 2005, which enhanced national security tools to deal with refugees, the Bush Administration was ineffectual on the immigration question. During the 2005-2006 period, conservatives in the House attempted to pass a bill which would have made illegal entry into the country a felony, only to be blocked by institutionalist Senate Republicans.[208] The next two years saw a miserable effort to enact comprehensive immigration reform using a bill that would have offered amnesty for millions of aliens and an agricultural guest worker program in exchange for expanded indefinite detainment powers over migrants, some border fencing funding, declaration of English as the national language, and creation of a mandatory E-Verify system.[209] This legislation would ultimately fail due to political opposition, though the Secure Fence Act of 2006 provided partial fencing along the border zone. On the executive side, despite his self-proclaimed role as an enforcer of employer penalties under the IRCA, DHS secretary Michael Chertoff backed off a crackdown on businesses after facing some public relations blowback in 2007.[210] Barack Obama's second term saw a concerted effort to revisit the immigration question through the Gang of Eight project in the U.S. Senate. To their credit, conservatives did stand firm on the amnesty question, preventing the law from ever going to Obama's desk by lining up opposition in the House.

The aftermath of this event would be seen with Donald Trump's successful presidential campaign founded on the specific matter of illegal immigration. Trump is the only president in recent memory to aggressively pursue migration using the full array of options, something which prior pro-business leaders would not deign to do. The combination of his travel ban directed at the Middle East, enhanced border enforcement, national emergency declaration to move wall construction funds, and scrutiny of the legal migration system had exceptionally positive results. One estimate holds that legal immigration alone dropped 49 percent during his term of office,[211] achieving something previously unthinkable by modern politicians. Part of the trend was no doubt influenced by the Coronavirus travel restrictions, but it still stands in contrast to the incredible failure of prior administrations to preserve a reasonable policy on the entry debate. If anything, Trump's greatest shortcoming on the matter was that his executive actions did not survive for a second term, and the lack of accompanying legislative change was certainly unhelpful.

Speaking of senatorial schemes, the first two years of the Trump presidency revealed how problematic legislative solutions have become. Paul Ryan may be labeled a "globalist" by conservatives, but he did allow two major provisions to pass the House.[212] The first was called Kate's Law, which would have drastically increased mandatory sentences for illegal aliens who commit violent crimes. Another was legislation designed to defund immigrant sanctuary cities, a major blow to Leftist conspiracies against the American worker. Sadly however, Mitch McConnell played his institutionalist role well, refusing to bring the bills up for a vote, or consider changing the filibuster rules to easily enact them. A further item proposed in the Senate itself was the RAISE Act, which would have established a more logical points-based system for legal migration, emphasizing skill sets and education level. Once again, McConnell failed to do his duty to the country, protecting the big business lobby and status quo procedures. While these important matters were left by the wayside, so-called "constitutional conservative" Senator Mike Lee pushed through legislation in December 2020 to remove the 7 percent annual country-of-origin visa caps,[213] playing to the Big Tech lobby and its desire to flood America with low-cost South Asian IT workers. At least on migration issues, the legislature cannot be trusted.

VIII. Foreign Policy

The matter which most clearly depicts Conservatism's failure is foreign affairs. As we already know, the conservative movement and Republican Party were broadly non-interventionist until the tail end of the 1940s. This does not suggest the non-existence of factions which broke from the mainstay earlier; indeed, the Progressive Era produced figures like Henry Cabot Lodge, who backed the League of Nations treaty. Nevertheless, the 1940s marked an aggressive transition towards the adamant, obsequious neoconservative support both for entry into World War II and the conflicts which followed. As with the tradition of deferment towards liberal morality, conservatives allowed themselves to be dragged into the war on the back of Democrat pronouncements. The GOP overwhelmingly endorsed the Neutrality Acts signed by FDR, but took minimal action to prevent the president's slippery descent into joining the Second World War with his lend-lease agreements benefiting Britain. Crucial to recognizing the depth of this dynamic is the reaction of 1944 Republican presidential nominee Thomas Dewey to a revelation about Franklin Roosevelt's betrayal of the country. Dewey was given a report ahead of his 1944 presidential run suggesting Roosevelt had advanced knowledge of the Pearl Harbor attack, but refused to make it a campaign issue.[214] The war had already progressed so far that even the moderate conservative Dewey avoided telling the truth about its origins, and how FDR may have squandered thousands of American lives.

Conservative hesitancy to intervene abroad was hardly helped by the post-war infusion of two elements into the broader ideological fold. First off, disgruntled liberals began filtering into the right-wing, pushing its majority posturing to an interventionist footing. No doubt the process was aided in large means by the heavy Jewish background of many neoconservatives, who saw failure to confront Hitler earlier as a primary reason for the Holocaust. Their efforts received a boon in relation to the conservative movement at-large by the flourishing of "godless" communism through the Soviet Union and its assortment of satellite states across the globe. Right-wingers fearful of communist takeovers in the West now had reason to back more extensive foreign adventurism as a check on Soviet aggression.

Dissent existed on this particular line, yet it was isolated to a limited section of the coalition. One example would be the Old Right Senator Robert Taft, who had expressed skepticism towards involvement in World War II, the NATO alliance, and American engagement in Vietnam: "I have always felt that we should not attempt to fight Russia on the ground of the Continent of Europe any more than we should attempt to fight China on the Continent of Asia."[215] Taft's ideas managed to influence Dwight Eisenhower against deploying ground troops to Indochina,[216] but by the time of Nixon's administration Republicans had essentially abandoned traditional conservative foreign policy.

Another instance of criticism emanated from the libertarian Murray Rothbard, who notably supported States' Rights Dixiecrat Strom Thurmond over Republican Thomas Dewey for president in 1948 based on the latter's endorsement of "internationalist" and "statist" positions.[217] Rothbard was also critical of Barry Goldwater's rise, seeing the Arizona senator as a warmonger who shared the audacious proclivity for bombing communist countries with noted neoconservative philosopher Frank Meyer.[218]

Despite these hostilities, Conservatism failed to contain the internationalist wing's influence, as a rather brief overview of history since the 1960s shows us. While conservatives did not start the Vietnam War, through until the Ford Administration the conflict was waged, with strong Republican support. Richard Nixon campaigned on ending America's engagement in Vietnam, but actually intervened to prevent an early peace settlement in the late 1960s with hopes of receiving political benefit.[219] He proceeded to expand the war's scope by bombing Laos and Cambodia, elongating a crisis that would not end until the Fall of Saigon in 1975. Even more egregiously, Nixon threatened the Soviet Union with nuclear war if Moscow intervened to support Arab nations against Israel.[220]

Ronald Reagan supported the Vietnam War and was elected on a platform emphasizing "peace through strength", a rather opaque term masking neoconservative malevolence. Such a mentality translated into his funding of the radical Islamic (but anti-Soviet) resistance in Afghanistan, the 1983 Invasion of Grenada, provision of aid to Jonas Savimbi's anti-communist rebels in Angola, similar involvement in El Salvador, and the infamous Iran-Contra Affair, wherein National Security Council staffers defied federal law to fund anti-Marxist rebels in Nicaragua.

One can argue Bush Senior was not much better than his predecessor on the international front. Early in his single term, he authorized the invasion of Panama to remove dictator Manuel Noriega, who years before had been recruited as a CIA asset and paid during the former's tenure as CIA director, as well as the administration of Ronald Reagan. After Saddam Hussein invaded Kuwait in 1991, Bush launched a UN coalition to drive the Iraqis out of the country and secure oil resources. It's worth appreciating that Bush had been involved in an earlier effort to militarily back Iraq during the 1980-1988 Iran-Iraq War, providing resources to a country that both he and his son would later confront.

Under the presidency of Bill Clinton, the weight of Israel began to fall heavily on national policy. Clinton initially opposed Republican Al D'Amato's 1995 legislative proposal which would have ended all economic ties between the United States and Iran,[221] but after the American oil company Conoco was chosen by the government in Tehran to develop the Sirri oil fields, things changed. Aggressive lobbying by the World Jewish Congress and the American-Israeli Political Action Committee (AIPAC) resulted in the issuance of two executive orders by Clinton that deep-sixed the deal.[222] Congress followed this up by passing the Iran-Libya Sanctions Act with overwhelming Republican support, applying penalties to companies making large investments in either country.[223] Both the cause of peace and American economic interests were forced to come second to Israeli priorities, and yet Israel's government took no action to end economic transactions between the Jewish State and Iran,[224] continuing to benefit while disadvantaging America.

The ascension of George W. Bush to presidential status in 2001 only worsened matters. Bush Jr. campaigned on a humble foreign policy before turning around and endorsing radical nation-building efforts in the Middle East. He was influenced here by the neoconservative Project For a New American Century think tank, and sympathetic members of his cabinet, including Donald Rumsfeld, Paul Wolfowitz, Condoleezza Rice, and John Bolton. Bush Jr. responded to the 9/11 attacks by invading Afghanistan and doing battle against the same Islamic fundamentalists supported by Reagan and Bush Senior against the Soviet Union. Afghanistan would morph into a 20-year conflict costing trillions of wealth and thousands of lives before ending in dramatic failure as the Taliban overthrew a liberal republican regime and reinstated their traditional government.

Bush Jr. went on to ignite a second war based on mostly deceptive terms, this time targeting the aging Saddam Hussein and his alleged nuclear stockpile. In foolish fashion, the invasion force disbanded Sunni-dominated Baath Party government structures, including the Iraqi Army and police services. The result was a bloody civil war between disenfranchised Sunnis and a new Shia/Kurd-led national government, along with assorted militias. Notably, Bush's mission against terrorism did not extend to the invasion of Saudi Arabia, where most of the 9/11 hijackers originated, and a state known for sponsoring terror campaigns around the world. Furthermore, it escaped no shrewd person that Bush's move against Saddam took pressure off the Iraqi leader's prime adversary, Israel.[225] That countless Bush advisers and associated think tank lobbyists were Zionists may be telling, though of course such an observation is outrageous and offensive.

Nevertheless, the Zionist Paul Wolfowitz served at the Defense Department, where he advocated an invasion of Iraq as early as September 15th, 2001.[226] He was supported in his neoconservative views over the years by an assortment of media talking heads, such as Robert Kagan of the Project For a New American Century, Bill Kristol of *The Weekly Standard*, Charles Krauthammer (who implicitly identified himself as an Israeli)[227], Michael Medved, Norman Podhoretz, and even the then-younger Ben Shapiro. Jonah Goldberg of the *National Review* was an especially grotesque example, with his pompous suggestion that America should occasionally invade a weaker country simply to show global dominance.[228] Notable is the fact that none of these characters served in the military themselves, and yet they have no problem sending young white, black, and Hispanic Americans to die for corrupt political causes. In doing so they embody an observation once made by Adam Smith, the famed economist:

> "In great empires the people who live in the capital, and in the provinces remote from the scene of action, feel, many of them, scarce any inconveniency from the war; but enjoy, at their ease, the amusement of reading in the newspapers the exploits of their own fleets and armies. To them this amusement compensates the small difference between the taxes which they pay on account of the war, and those which they had been accustomed to pay in time of peace. They are commonly dissatisfied with the return of peace, which puts an end to their amusement, and to a thousand visionary hopes of conquest and national glory from a longer continuance of war."[229]

Our reaction to such behavior need not imply the utter denial of any political voice for Zionists, yet the conservative movement must cease tethering foreign policies to favor not merely cordial relations with Israel, but in fact the ultranationalist ends of leaders in the Israeli Likud Party. We see the degree of subversion when arch-Rightist, former House Majority Leader Dick Armey notes that, "my No. 1 priority in foreign policy is to protect Israel", while his successor Tom DeLay described himself as, "an Israeli at heart."[230] The Tea Party firebrand Michele Bachmann later labeled Israel as "our greatest ally" while arguing against foreign aid cuts to the nation, preferring instead that Iraq and Libya, whose Israeli-hostile governments were overthrown by the U.S., pay reparations to Washington, D.C.[231] Like-minded actors on both sides even managed to defeat a 2007 legislative requirement for the president to gain approval before attacking Iran,[232] ensuring preemptive strikes would not be hindered by the democratic process.

The phenomenon was glaringly visible in the 2014-2015 drama surrounding a nuclear deal negotiation with Iran. The Obama Administration had been attempting to reach an agreement with the government in Tehran over strong objections from the House Republican majority and then-prime minister of Israel Benjamin Netanyahu. Disregarding constitutional traditions which vest foreign affairs powers in the president, Speaker John Boehner invited Netanyahu to speak before Congress In January 2015 without consulting Obama, at the same time threatening passage of a sanctions bill to derail the nuclear negotiations.[233]

Netanyahu had been spreading ludicrous fears about Iran for years, including with his infamous 2012 speech before the UN, where he held up a cartoon diagram of a bomb "in-progress" to illustrate Iran's closeness to a nuclear weapon. What's more disturbing is the reaction of self-described conservatives beyond Boehner's invitation. In March 2015, 47 Republican senators led by the neoconservative Tom Cotton published an open letter to the leaders of Iran wherein they implied any agreement concluded without congressional ratification would be seen as a mere executive action with no long-term foundations. Though Cotton was speaking from a position of constitutional accuracy, the rather rudimentary approach of the letter made it unnecessary aside from an ulterior motive to serve as a voice of Israel against the deal. Perhaps he was influenced by receiving $960,250 in campaign advertising support for his 2014 election campaign from the Emergency Committee For Israel, a pressure group headed by Bill Kristol.[234] To suggest a conflict of influence here would be wise, but also garner accusations of racism.

Sadly, Trump built on said Zionist militancy after ascending to the presidency in 2017. Despite his claims of being an American nationalist and non-interventionist, the president followed the lead of his countless Jewish advisers by officially designating Jerusalem as the capital of Israel, effectively endorsing a pro-Israeli position in the struggle over Palestinian statehood. He went on to withdraw from the Iranian nuclear deal and applied sanctions to the government of Tehran, reverting America's posture to one of hawkish neoconservatism. Trump would also recognize Israeli sovereignty over the Golan Heights, a region formerly belonging to Syria but occupied by Israel since 1967.

On the domestic front, the 45th president signed the Never Again Act, expanding education on the Holocaust by allocating $10 million for a project which already has no shortage of exposure on television and in the classroom. Executive action around the same time attempted to expand Title VI protections to Jews on college campuses which receive federal funding, though the move was widely interpreted as an attempt to delimit criticism of Israel's government. Perhaps more disturbing is the policy of Texas under Trump ally Greg Abbott, who signed a law in 2017 barring state contract bidding by any company engaged in the Boycott, Divestment, and Sanctions (BDS) movement directed against Israel.[235] The grander consequence was felt by special needs instructor Bahia Amawi, who after ten years teaching for a Texas school district was let go because she failed to sign an oath in her contract promising not to support BDS.[236] That pro-Israel policy would reach so deeply into the local fluctuations of politics indicates a serious stranglehold by the Middle Eastern nation over our lawmakers.

Foreign Policy Reform

At bare minimum, salvation of the conservative position will require both sacrifices and honesty. America cannot continue conjuring up excuses to fund overseas defense contractors to incredible lengths by engaging abroad where no genuine national interest resides. If the issue is satisfying donors, programs can be redirected to the home front, for instance by farming out contractors who can build the border barrier, or deploying defensive technologies which support homeland security. Thirst for war-specific measures might be sated by an actual war against the drug cartels, with use of precision strikes on their compounds in Mexico, as Trump once suggested.[237] Other monies can be deployed to create regional economic alliances in Africa and the Caribbean as a check on China's expanding foothold there. What is not needed ought to simply cease being spent, as financial security is unquestionably tied to national security.

A provision of truth, no matter how difficult, is also in order with regards to our foreign interactions. For too long, indeed since the end of World War II, Conservatism has been bound up in the fear of being called a bad name over not supporting the national interests of Israel. This must end. No more is the Jewish State weak and under the auspices of primitive technological conditions; it boasts one of the highest living standards in the Middle East and has a nuclear arsenal larger than the oft-cited threat of North Korea. Whatever opponents pose danger to its existence can be more than handled without American backing at the frontal or silent partner positions. Only when conservatives embrace realist viewpoints shall we be able to proceed and evade the mistakes of the past. As the half-Jewish Barry Goldwater once noted, "I don't worry about Israel when I go to sleep at night. I worry about the U.S. Constitution, which I've sworn to uphold—not Israel's constitution, not that of Saudi Arabia, Lebanon, or anybody else in the Middle East or the world."[238]

IX. What Can Be Done

It would irresponsible to delineate the flaws of an ideology and then leave it wallowing on the historical plane, absent any suggestions for improvement. I suspect in the case of Conservatism a clear vision must be displayed if any hope can be had for the future. The stopwatch has run too far ahead to accommodate the sluggish legislating and speech-giving which right-wing actors have advocated for years within the confines of the safe liberal system; creative and decisive action must be pursued to rescue the nation, regardless of how threatening it may seem to established conservative theoreticians. In some cases these ideas will actually canter agreeably alongside Rightist norms, while others may seem to stretch the bars of belief and lawyered acceptability. Our mission must be to charge on regardless, powered by the intense love of country so long denied by the adapting, curmudgeon philosophy of the American Right.

If you bother to ask established conservatives what *can* be done, they invariably fall along a handful of castrated lines. According to former Senator Jeff Flake, the solution rests with a steady return to values and principles as opposed to short-term interests or political expediency.[239] He cites the late Barry Goldwater to grant a similar perspective:

> "There are occasions when we have elevated men and political parties to power that promised to restore limited government and then proceeded, after their election, to expand the activities of government. Broken promises are not the major causes of our trouble. *Kept* promises are. All too often we have put men in office who have suggested spending a little more on this, a little more on that, who have proposed a new welfare program, who have thought of another variety of 'security'. We have taken the bait, preferring to put off to another day the recapture of freedom and the restoration of our constitutional system."[240]

Goldwater has much wisdom to offer us, though even he conceded that freedom should only prevail in concert with the maintenance of social order.[241] Regrettably, modern Rightists continue harkening the death of Conservatism and conservative values in any recognizable form because they defer so strongly to "the system" without that creative spark needed for genuine restoration. A good example here would be the polemicist Charlie Sykes, who aggressively appeals for a return to the tenets of classical liberalism in response to the "authoritarian nationalism" of Trump.[242] For Sykes, this means following the behavior of apparently "consistent" figures like Bill Kristol, John Podhoretz, David Frum, and Jonah Goldberg,[243] all neoconservative activists who favor internationalism and Arab World regime change benefiting Israel.

Even a skeptic of the recent national populist trends must concede that Sykes is woefully misguided with his prescriptions. The simple fact remains that the Republic has become more threatened as a direct result of embracing liberalism, and in particular with no limitations to the equalitarian principle buttressing it. The Founders were wise enough to understand the imperative of paternalism as a means of preserving freedom for society at-large. They thus restricted voting rights not merely to one race, but members of that group who were established in society and owned property. Loose enfranchisement to endorse some point about individualism never seriously crossed from their minds to the ink and paper of the Constitution.

No, we must cease burying heads in hands and wistfully hoping for a return to the olden values absent any realistic strategy; the time has come to awaken the national will for something bolder. To certain minds, the pivot immediately points to a shadowy era of the past where rules are tossed out and all traditions disregarded, yet nothing could be further from the truth. We are lucky enough to possess a Constitution that quite capably affords allowance for the deft action so pleaded for by the present state of America. Through these tools Conservatism can actually be given a fighting chance, and perhaps rerouted into the system of safeguards that once made it viable.

Using the Legislative Option

Our first strike involves appropriate use of the legislature to ratify conservative protections. From a traditionalist standpoint, the legislative filibuster might seem perfectly natural, protecting minority rights against the tenets of mob rule. Indeed, Jeff Flake employs such Madisonian logic regarding the legislature while castigating Donald Trump for desiring a return to simple majority functionality in the Senate.[244] According to Flake, this would result in a one-sided, "I win, you lose" form of politics against the constitutional convictions of the Founding. Perhaps he is right, but there should be no excuse for the travesty of inaction that conservatives have tolerated for years regarding legislative reform. When the political procedure is allowed to play out, with deal-making as some sainted token of recognition, the outcome is invariably human suffering on a large scale, along with continued descent into political oblivion.

It is thus imperative for conservatives to begin appreciating how the lawmaking process works, because alternatively the option will be continual stagnation. A future Republican Congress and unified presidency should deftly utilize the reconciliation process to force through their ideals, defying the institutional conservatives of earlier days. A simple majority vote can be used to promulgate spending in areas of necessity. Funding the construction of a border barrier should not for instance be held up over many months when it can be readily deployed by basic legislative gamesmanship. Partial civil service reform falls into the same category, with cuts or restructuring being reasonable options on the horizon. Supposing the parliamentarian rules against inclusion of certain items in the legislation, the Senate leadership can move to dismiss that office-holder and replace them with a being more malleable towards creative improvements. The country need not otherwise float for ages in perpetual gridlock just to protect dim arguments about restraint.

Reconciliation might also be used to cut out large swaths of the existing spending for needless cabinet departments. Conservatives have, for instance, railed against the evils inherent to Section 8 housing and its federal agency administrator, the Department of Housing and Urban Development. Nevertheless, they offer up only modest internal reforms on the bureaucratic level, and fall behind arguments of bipartisanship when it comes to appropriation cuts. The result is that no substantive reductions in the actual size or scope of government have been achieved despite decades of declaration in favor the same ideal.

To grasp the contrast between such institutionalism and proactive creativity, observe the antics of the Schumer Senate during the early months of 2021. Instead of lazily embracing tradition like the typical Rightist senator, with a maximum of two reconciliation bills across two fiscal years, Democrats lobbied the Senate Parliamentarian to agree that the narrow majority rule can be used on far more occasions.[245] This allowed them to enact the American Rescue Plan on a mere 50-49 vote in the Senate, and threaten similar use for Biden's massive infrastructure bill. The latter piece was eventually ratified with Republican help, but Democrat tenacity would have almost certainly brought it to success absent the other party.

A natural follow-up here was of course the Build Back Better Act, a $3.5 trillion dollar legislative package designed to drastically expand liberal policies on a national scale. Although initially slated for passage, the defection of West Virginia's Joe Manchin caused a slowdown assumed by many conservatives to be the death knell for Biden's agenda. But while Republican politicians simply concluded that was the end of the process until after the 2022 midterms, Democrats under Schumer chose to bide their time, and continued searching for Manchin's price. The struggle culminated in a surprise decision to revisit the legislation in August 2022, after the GOP had been tricked into voting for a major semiconductor subsidy bill due to an assumption that social spending would not be retried.[246] Manchin came on board and allowed passage of the Inflation Reduction Act on a 51-50 vote. Customs and tradition did not matter. The Democrats were determined to advance their cause, and simply needed to find the right set of terms. Their methods remain a roadmap for aspirational conservative reform.

The Executive Will To Act

Before delving into possible executive solutions to our crisis, it is important to revisit the nature of state power itself. Key to conservative reticence here is the limited government principles they tend to hold. When finally confronted with the realities of power and the ability to use it, such actors shrink from the moment, becoming terrified of how decisive action could irreparably damage government structures, or perhaps at some later point be turned against them. Said risks are not foreign to any political reality in our nation, yet using them as an excuse is to goad the opposite side into crossing that line first.

According to Niccolo Machiavelli, politics is about the struggle for power between men.[247] What this translates to in the brutal realm of statecraft is the need to project strength and weaken adversaries in such a manner that the ruthless actor retains control and can prosecute his agenda continuously – not simply for a short intermission period. Traditional conservative politicians dislike the uncompromising suggestion brought forth here because they prefer to imagine both sides will honor the limits of the system providing each acts in a sincere manner. Furthermore, the assumption of defeat and minority status carried by the bulk of Rightists, where they are a "silent majority" afraid to speak too loudly against a Leftist horde, terrifies them into weakly prosecuting state power, which itself causes cultural and political catastrophe.

We may be able to assuage the paranoid souls by turning to Machiavelli once more. The Florentine theorist observed that power struggles are reserved primarily for a small class of "ruler-type" men, in contrast to the ruled masses who exercise relatively little effective control.[248] The vast majority of that latter population can be corralled into support for a cause providing they find themselves impressed by demonstrations of firm action: "There is nothing more certain to appease a popular tumult, and reduce the people to reason, than the interposition of some wise person of authority among them [...]".[249] Citing the example of a barbarian invasion threatening Rome, Machiavelli describes how individual citizens are ready to criticize the actions of their leaders, but in isolation and facing possible death, fear causes them to obey the state. [250] Put otherwise, the state itself precedes the written law, and creates legal codes based on its authority, rather than being bound to them in a subservient, limited way.[251]

In the present American context, conservative actors have access to a Constitution which actually affords great explicit and assumed powers to the president, if he has the courage to fully invoke them. The latter dynamic, embodied by the Will to Act principle, stands as the best chance to save the Republic and resist national enemies. For Rightists the challenge will be safeguarding the legitimacy of state power insofar as they wield it.[252] Left-wingers fully comprehend this virtue, which explains their violent attempts to undermine Trump's authority with stylized "Resistance" propaganda, and the widespread riots showcased in 2020. Once Biden assumed the presidency however, progressives quickly set about turning the erstwhile "illegitimate" state into a powerful weapon to subdue their ideological opponents. Long-preserved hopes by the Right that its good behavior could somehow elicit reciprocity from the Left proved to be utterly unfounded.

A first principle when examining the use of unilateral authority is to realize basic structural nature. Governmental systems may thrive on the narrow basis of popular mandates, yet democracy itself creates conditions where a designated minority will exist, disillusioned by the failure of their particular candidate to take power. Our goal as practitioners of statecraft must then entail securing positive impressions from *enough* of the populace, and not following the assumption that all citizens are intellectually reasonable creatures capable of exercising power themselves. Recall Machiavelli's theory about how the majority class is intended to be ruled; the objective is not to turn each citizen into a policy wonk, but rather let them give way to the sense that a specific cause is just. Indeed, democratic political legitimacy has more to do with perceptions about the system embodying the people's values,[253] and not obscure questions of how one chooses to strictly interpret a law. Applied to our world today, where Republicans struggle to win national popular vote majorities and glide by through the Electoral College, the executive model becomes even more crucial.

Adopting such a position is obviously bound to upset libertarians and classical liberals, who will cite John Locke to warn of the dangers inherent to centralized government. But Locke was a man of his time, concerned with the tendency of European monarchs to use their power in a retaliatory manner against dissenting figures, seizing property or banishing those opponents from the kingdom. He concluded that the use of a majoritarian system would place checks on the king's ability in these regards, naturally because the voting class was still led by property-owning elites. The conceptions he advanced regarding natural law were another layer of defense, imagining an elevated, universal authority establishing rights that monarchs should be prepared to respect.

Locke was not however a committed libertarian devoted to castrating the strength of the state. Like his ideological descendant Thomas Jefferson, he recognized the importance of a strong, central figure capable of acting decisively and "without a rule"[254] to serve the national interest. An executive would remain under said conceptions because it ensured the preservation of the system in extreme events. He notes:

> "This power to act according to discretion, for the public good, without the prescription of the law, and sometimes even against it, is that which is

called prerogative: for since in some governments the lawmaking power is not always in being, and is usually too numerous, and so too slow, for the dispatch requisite to execution; and because also it is impossible to foresee, and so by laws to provide for, all accidents and necessities that may concern the public, or to make such laws as will do no harm, if they are executed with an inflexible rigour, on all occasions, and upon all persons that may come in their way; therefore there is a latitude left to the executive power, to do many things of choice which the laws do not prescribe."[255]

Such "latitude" is precisely why presidential power was not put down in detail on constitutional paper by the Founding Fathers. These were men who realized that the fallen state of the world could easily create conditions wherein survival of the nation and civil government required more swift action than a corrupt legislature could begin to muster. They did not wish to see the country completely hamstrung with regional debates and influence-peddling to where any possibility of sane progress for the country as a whole would be shut down.

As they wrote the Constitution, the Founders wrestled over how much power precisely should be vested in a central government, if any at all. Figures like Edmund Randolph and James Madison attempted to advance the Virginia Plan, a model which mandated the president be elected by Congress itself and exist as little more than an administrative figurehead to enforce the law, with his cabinet being controlled by legislators to varying degrees as well.[256] Those familiar with arch-libertarians in the modern day will often hear them characterize the presidency in such a light, as a weak office designed more for caretaking than to pursue bold decisions unilaterally.

Alexander Hamilton on the other hand favored a presidential governor aligned with the English monarchy in structure, highlighted by his observation that "energy in the executive is the leading character of good government".[257] Such a figure would be chosen by electors representing the voters and be ensconced for life absent removal by impeachment.[258] He would be like our president the executor of laws, but with an added weapon in the shape of an absolute veto, without possibility of legislative override. But the final model selected for the governing document was a compromise which distributed power between the three branches without falling prey to those anti-national forces seeking effectively a confederal solution to the governing question.

What the Founders did wisely include in the original Constitution was presidential capacity to go above and beyond the indolent legislature in assuming responsibility for critical matters concerning the national interest. The president's role as the sole figure elected by the entire nation was key to this conception because it gave him a status as the singular voice of the people, unbound by strict regional interests and that deal-making corruption complimentary to them. Critical here is Article II of the Constitution, which lays out broad and surreptitiously vague terms of presidential power. Not only does this brief segment enshrine the president as a unique office holder in the United States, distinct from the legislative actors often eager to snipe at him; it also showcases a dramatic theory of power in moments of crisis. Most notably, we have Section 3:

> He shall from time to time give to the Congress Information on the State of the Union, and recommend to their Consideration such Measures as he shall judge necessary and expedient; he may, on extraordinary Occasions, convene both Houses, or either of them, and in Case of Disagreement between them, with Respect to the Time of Adjournment, he may adjourn them to such Time as he shall think proper; he shall receive Ambassadors and other public Ministers; he shall take Care that the Laws be faithfully executed, and shall Commission all the Officers of the United States.

Pay attention to the language regarding adjournment, and specifically, "to such Time as he shall think proper". That ability, which has not been tested yet by a commander-in-chief, can well be interpreted as placing the presidency over the legislature in cases of conflict or chaos. With full constitutional integrity, the executive can essentially shut down another branch's primary operations and act in its stead as the undisputed government of the United States. Had the libertarian-leaning individuals at the Founding won out, such language would almost assuredly not exist, for it invites the political emasculation of popular representatives by a single figure. Whether a competent activist conservative president could employ the tactic to demonstrate domination over wide swaths of policy is an open question for consideration.

The relative flexibility of the president is logical if we view him as being able to react to majors affairs of state. Should the country be at risk of an impending attack by China, for instance, we would not want 535 congressmen and senators getting together for a televised debate in order to grandstand about their personal opinions on the matter. That would project weakness and lack of unity, two factors a strong leader will ably trample. Instead, the president can move with deftness to order up a defense of the nation. Should his actions perhaps verge on the territory of questionably legal, or clearly illegal behavior, they can be excused on the basis that crucial values of the Republic are at stake. Even Thomas Jefferson, popular among libertarians for his smaller government persuasions, had the following to say about laws:

> "A strict observance of the written laws is doubtless *one* of the high duties of a good citizen, but it is not *the highest*. The laws of necessity, of

self-preservation, of saving our country when in danger, are of higher
obligation. To lose our country by a scrupulous adherence to written law,
would be to lose the law itself, with life, liberty, property and all those
who are enjoying them with us; thus absurdly sacrificing the end to the
means."[259]

Here we see how the traditionalist imperative must at times be relaxed in order to
pursue moral objectives, including salvation of the country at-large. It does not
matter if the letter of laws cannot be always followed perfectly, as difficult
decisions by the executive are justified by sheer force of will, and with the
approval of the public. Americans elect the president, giving him a political and
spiritual mandate to safeguard their well-being now and in future, regardless of
what squabbling legislators or curmudgeonly judges presume to say. They remain
creatures of a decadent system which attempts to place unrealistic observance of
impartiality above the possibility of national renewal.

Historical Legal Foundations

To comprehend how sickly hypocritical the opposing, institutionalist viewpoint is,
consider a history of decisions by the Supreme Court versus the Legislative
Branch and Presidency. As we are brought up to understand, the president is
coequal with the Supreme Court and Congress, and yet jurists, including
institutional conservatives, regularly flip-flop over the principle to the detriment of
national salvation. For instance, few would question the primacy of the president
in the matter of foreign affairs or the military; this role is clearly spelled out in
Article II, which directs him to engage in treaties and serve as the highest
commander of our armed forces. The Senate must ratify such international
agreements, however, and Congress as a whole is expected to make a declaration
of war when the time calls for it.

Regardless, the legislature often relies on diabolical means to cede its own
responsibility to the president on unpleasant matters. In response to the conduct of
the Vietnam War and associated air campaigns in Southeast Asia, Congress
enacted the War Powers Resolution of 1973, a dramatic piece of legislation
attempting to reign in presidential unilateralism by requiring him to notify the
legislature within 48 hours of ordering armed forces into combat. A grand total of
90 days are allowed to elapse between deployment and withdrawal before the
president must seek an Authorization for the Use of Military Force (AUMF) for
continued action from Congress. The term "authorization" is critical here because
it permits cowardly legislators to wash their hands of a difficult war declaration
vote. More disturbingly, the legislation did not act to amend the Constitution, but
rather attempted to transfer Congress' duty with a mere federal law.

Unsurprisingly, the measure has been disregarded numerous times with little legal repercussion for the commander-in-chief.

The Legislative Branch followed up with the Congressional Budget and Impoundment Control Act of 1974, a law of questionable origins that worked to diminish Richard Nixon's attempts at using impoundment as a form of unilateral budget cuts. Impoundment is a practice through which the president refuses to release earmarked funds put forth by Congress due to his disagreement with the use of those monies for various reasons. What makes the bill strange is its assumption of an ability on the part of the president not openly permitted or prohibited by the Constitution itself. Article I Section 9 Clause 7 undoubtedly makes Congress the king of appropriations, yet the Presidency remains responsible for executing laws and *administering* the state. If this is the case, then why should he not possess the capacity to choose how monies are spent, if at all? Appropriation is at best the provision of funds, but blockades of presidential impoundment are nothing more than a cynical attempt by Congress to keep taxpayer funds flowing without addressing the larger issue of national bankruptcy brought on by their own actions. Conservative lawyers should be readily examining the law for a legal challenge precisely on such constitutional terms.

Not to be outmoded, Congress made an attempt in the 1990s to rein in spending by enacting a line-item veto for use by the president. Bill Clinton would use the tool (a federal law) to promulgate his planned spending reductions and bring the budget closer to surplus, but in 1998 it was struck down by a conservative/liberal alliance on the Supreme Court, with the argument that the law amounted to a unilateral veto power on the part of the president. Here the leaps in judicial logic are difficult to explain away. Congress can apparently make laws which restrict the president's administrative power based on a dubious reading of the Constitution, cede authority to him on matters of war (in violation of the legislative prerogative), but then expand other areas entirely. Meanwhile, the supposedly co-equal presidency must act with toothless energy in response to such evident abuse. Anyone of righteous spirit can see how contradictory and dangerous the present model is. A country faces countless threats and financial ruin, but only a capricious and compromised body can be permitted to solve the problem.

Executive Order Dynamism

Luckily, a brighter path does exist. We might start with the essence of the executive order. In earlier days, these edicts were seen to be at best temporary measures, subject to scrutiny and review by the judiciary, or repeal by a future president. Over time they have morphed into effective peers with federal law, backed not only by court rulings but also the tacit consent of the nation. In 1976, as the government shook from years of scandal and growing public distrust, Gerald Ford issued Order 11905, which explicitly prohibited any member of the U.S. government from engaging in political assassinations around the world.[260] By 2001 however, Congress had moved to expand the president's power to kill through legislation, again on shaky constitutional grounds, but it was in 2013 when things truly ascended. That year Barack Obama's Justice Department released a memo claiming unfettered powers to target individuals – including American citizens – for assassination.[261] Notably, the courts did not rush in to stop Obama's schemes, but have in fact largely supported extreme national defense powers on the part of the president.

Still, skeptics of further action will use the foreign affairs excuse to argue executive action is limited to that realm, and here march straight against the painful developments of modern legal theory. Though such posturing might have worked in the midst of earlier days, recent court decisions have struck at the foundation of this vague, "zone of the president" idea. Quite notably, Barack Obama's 2015 unilateral action on DACA immigration policy pushed the envelope irrevocably in an authoritarian direction. Conservatives mounted a series of legal challenges to block the move on constitutional grounds, only to be rebuffed by a split Supreme Court, which allowed the program to stay in place. It's worth noting that DACA had not been formalized in federal legislation, yet the usual supporters of legislative supremacy did not break on that specific angle.

Some years later, President Trump moved to rescind DACA, following the traditional custom of executive orders being short-term and inferior to Congressional statutes. The Plural Left naturally sued, and in the summer of 2020 John Roberts led a narrow majority in refusing to accept the rescission, employing a clownish justification that the Trump Administration had not followed legal guidelines by providing "a reasoned explanation for its action."[262] Similar legal maneuvering was used by Roberts to prevent the inclusion of a citizenship question on the U.S. Census the year prior,[263] torpedoing an important tool meant to preserve the American nation-state against globalist subversion.

While adherence of the justices to legalistic perversions might appear to limit presidential power, they were in fact *solidifying* Obama's unilateral move as having force approximate to a federal law. Trump could not simply remove the program conjured out of thin air, at least not absent a process comparable to Congress voting for legislative repeal. This raises the inevitable query of what else might stand through force of an executive order alone, especially considering the supposed equality of the three governmental branches.

We saw a partial preview of the answer with Joe Biden's executive actions on the COVID-19 vaccine mandate. Based heavily on OSHA regulations, Biden issued a nationwide order requiring injection of an experimental vaccine into millions of workers, on threat of fines or employment dismissal. Legal challenges were slow to advance, and the failure of the Supreme Court to issue an emergency injunction blocking the president meant that countless Americans had no choice but to bend the knee in order to save their jobs and put food on the table. In other terms, Biden was incredibly effective at achieving his goal and cowing millions of his dissenters, regardless of whatever outcome materialized. When the Supreme Court finally issued a stay order for Biden's OSHA mandate in January 2022, they surreptitiously left open the possibility of a more flexible mandate for high-risk workers, [264] and permitted companies to enforce private mandates in the workplace. A narrow majority also sided with Biden's separate mandate for federal health facilities, allowing unilateral coercion of around 17 million people.

Scaling Back Government

The aforementioned constitutional foundations sanction great leeway by a future conservative leader, whether Trump or another actor, to prosecute a president-driven return to the lost traditions of the Republic. Already in 2017, an advisor to Trump's Domestic Policy Council issued a memo noting, "Article II executive power gives the president inherent authority to dismiss any federal employee. This implies civil service legislation and union contracts impeding that authority are unconstitutional."[265] The following year, Trump advanced the cause through a series of executive actions which weakened union protections for federal workers.[266] The Trump Administration also challenged status quo protections for administrative law judges in national bureaucracies, resulting in a narrowly-written Supreme Court decision wherein conservative justices implied the Founding Fathers would have seen all federal government officials as being subject to the presidential appointments power.[267]

Stephen Miller, Trump's advisor on immigration, demonstrated concurrent zeal for the trend by reassigning dissenting pro-migration advocates from key government departments and programs critical to national policy goals.[268] White House Presidential Personnel Office head John McEntee did the same in 2020 by employing his powers to remove political appointees who were seen as disloyal to the president's conservative agenda,[269] beginning a process only cut short by the results of the November election.

Looking forward, the creative possibilities realized during Trump's first term have already attracted fascination from concerned Leftists who fear what a second iteration might bring. At the core of his agenda would be reinstatement of the "Schedule F" order first implemented in October 2020.[270] Under its purview, as many as 50,000 federal workers can be released from employment based upon their relative status in the civil service and lack of long-term job protections.

Given the malevolence exhibited by bureaucrats during Trump's initial time in office, there is good reason to use the tool as a means of ridding the state of subversive actors who cannot be trusted to faithfully and impartially advance national objectives. President Eisenhower led such a campaign in the 1950s that resulted not only in 10,000 federal workers being fired, but also the professional defenestration of at least 600 liberal academics nationwide, and a revocation of pensions for Leftists.[271] Pursuing similar actions in the present day would save taxpayer money and assist with the march towards conservative reform.

In terms of broader federal spending problems, the journey becomes complicated. While it is aspirational to imagine the possibilities of moderate compromise, the entire political system has become so polarized by media and gerrymandering that no realistic fiscal solution will emanate from Congress, and certainly not in time to avoid financial catastrophe. Too many representatives and senators have their hands in the honeypot of pet projects, federal grants, and corporate or union subsidies. They cannot be incentivized to cut spending because any tough position would naturally endanger their district, state, or reelection prospects. A different path is necessary.

As fate would have it, the map leads us to a revisiting of impoundment as a means of getting the national purse under control. The basis for such a mechanism lies with the Unitary Executive Theory, a conception of the Constitution under which the president exerts full control over the Executive Branch and its bureaucracy, not merely as a timid caretaker, but the active and unquestioned leader, accountable in his role only to the popular mandate of the voters, and not legislative power-sharing.[272] Strong backing exists at minimum for the basic unitary idea at the conservative Federalist Society, whose members were closely tied to both the Bush Jr. and Trump administrations. In the case of Society member Bill Barr, his application to become attorney general under Trump was prefaced by a column in which he noted that the president, "alone is the executive branch."[273] This builds upon a layman's understanding of executive power by the 45th president himself, when he claimed, "It's a thing called Article II. . . . It gives me all of these rights at a level that nobody has ever seen before."[274]

Grandiose declarations aside, if we except the formulations of the unitary concept on the core merits, there is no logical or legal reason why the president cannot refuse to release funds allocated by Congress, which is supposed to be a co-equal branch. Forcing him to live under the tyranny of corrupt representatives implies a feeble, figurehead-like legislative creature warned against by Gouverneur Morris during the Founding era.[275] Instead, a conservative president must assert executive power and declare that large swaths of the federal budget are on hold, "frozen" if you will, and thus not able to contribute to the fiscal damnation of America. In the face of court rulings or legislative retaliation he must stand strong, refusing to surrender clear authority over the management of the state and its iterations. Successful resistance could actually turn the practice into something of a bargaining chip; Congress will of course want money spent on its pet projects, but have to negotiate in good faith on the president's budgetary proposals rather than simply voting in overwhelming omnibus bills that violate constitutional prerogatives regarding the enactment of budgets.

Earnest theorists can rest easier by knowing that the process of legal evolution is already underway. Years ago, Alexis De Tocqueville predicted such a shift would come about, observing that the president possessed great power on the level of a regent, but was bound by circumstances which would adjust as the country expanded. National security in particular would contribute to this transformation until, "the executive government would assume an increased importance in proportion to the measures expected of it and to those which it would execute."[276]

A perfect example of the developing nature in the presidency is the first impeachment of Donald Trump. As many already know, the president came under fire for a July 2019 incident when he allegedly threatened to withhold foreign aid to Ukraine based on the conditionality of an investigation being launched there into the business dealings of Hunter Biden, the son of his eventual 2020 election rival. Much gnashing of teeth was had on both sides of the aisle over the affair, which came to a muted finish after the Senate voted to acquit Trump in February 2020. What the partisans failed to appreciate however was the way Trump radically expanded the impoundment power through his holding back of the $400 million package destined by congressional order to reach Ukraine. As a senior Democrat implied, failure to impeach and remove Trump would have the effect of ratifying the president's unilateral actions and turning him into something of a monarch beyond reproach.[277] That view would later be echoed by former National Security Advisor John Bolton, who saw the aborted conviction as empowering and vindicating Trump.[278]

Tackling The Federal Reserve

There are plenty of voices on the Plural Right who advocate not simply cutting spending, but indeed enacting a balanced budget amendment which might keep future drunken spenders at bay. While such a program has its merits, we should keep in mind that most proposals include an exception for times of war, rendering them effectively null. All politicians would have to do is continue the long-running "War on Terror" and thus avoid ever having to face cost restrictions under the terms of such an amendment. Alternatively, they might simply take spending off the books[279] and officially balance the budget while continuing to lead America into the depths of fiscal ruination. Greed is after all a difficult enemy to vanquish, especially when it can be sated using public money.

A better option would be to examine Federal Reserve policy and its propensity to result in endless money creation backed by no safe store of value. The Fed operates as a private institution under limited government oversight (itself a violation of the Constitution), and is widely seen to prop up swaths of the economy by injecting paper currency into the market, steadily defeating the hopes of conservatives who believe in currency circulation restrictions and sound money approaches. Such folks often call for a return to the Gold Standard, theorizing that such a move would reduce inflation and create barriers to the runaway spending prosecuted by both parties in Congress. Because paper money printed with gold backing is not allowed to exceed the total gold supplies of the issuing country, the large-scale cash infusions committed by the Fed and legislators in 2008 and 2020 would have supposedly never happened, preserving the value of the dollar over time.

The reality is less endearing, however. Gold's scarcity and popular appeal have not prevented it from falling prey to government price manipulation over the years, including outright inflationary actions.[280] It also complicates matters for those nations who may have even smaller supplies of precious metals, as they cannot likely expand their control unless more is discovered or somehow acquired. Perhaps a better option would be for the president to tie currency issuance to the nation's labor productivity and value-added GDP.[281] Doing so would break the hold of the central bank on inflationary debasement of the dollar, while delimiting congressional ability to keep the coffers filled with flimsy paper money. To further hammer at the Federal Reserve, the president might direct his Treasury secretary to print interest-free notes, gradually lifting the financial yoke and influence of the private bank over the lives of companies and American citizens.[282]

Cutting Immigration

Absent an aggressive reversal of the demographic invasion impacting our nation, Conservatism will be left to join that moderate-faced neoliberal cult which has dominated world politics for the last several decades. Achieving a victory on the legislative level seems improbable given current levels of polarization and corporate lobbying malevolence, so the executive option must be supreme. Here it will be imperative to have the appropriate staff on hand, and a creative understanding of the law. For one, the immensely corrupt Temporary Protective Status (TPS) program for refugees must be severely curtailed. Under its existing terms, vague claims of human rights violations are enough to trigger eligibility, even if the individuals benefiting cannot prove they are in credible danger. An effort was made to do just this by Stephen Miller which eliminated TPS coverage of 200,000 Salvadorans and 50,000 Haitians, along with thousands of Nicaraguans and Sudanese.[283] Acting USCIS head Ken Cuccinelli took related action on the matter by directing his subordinates to be skeptical of asylum justification claims.[284] Of course Miller's action on TPS was challenged on racial grounds by the ACLU, confirming the Plural Left's psychotic obsession with attempting to prove there is no demographic replacement narrative, despite supporting the same trend.

Other angles of effective redress involve implementation of bureaucratic rules on migration. Americans witnessed the early success of these methods with the Title 42 policy, which prevents access to the country by those who may have been exposed to a communicable disease elsewhere. Use of the health angle is critical because we have already seen the willingness of the Supreme Court to rule in favor of top-down protections if the setting is appropriately-designated. Requiring refugees to seek asylum in a safe third country adds layers to the mix by preventing their hysterical concerns from automatically leading to entrance into the United States, as opposed to some other place in Central America. The fashioning of the "public charge" rule heightens the stakes by making it unlikely for those liable to be placed on welfare to enter and become a burden. An expansion of the restrictions to encapsulate use of general government services would go a long way in reducing migration by ensuring only those fit to work and without dependents can gain passage.

Future leaders should take additional action by reviving older statutes which banned foreigners in certain localities from purchasing property,[285] thus making it difficult for them to put down roots on the sheer basis of possessing currency. Legislation of such nature has already been proposed in Florida,[286] though it is far too narrow and not applied to enough countries. The nation must be preserved for its people, and not simply anyone having a few dollars to spend.

The competent politico shall however note that these programmatic solutions will be viciously challenged in court by those preferring the pro-corporate, anti-national position. In point, Trump's decision to move federal funds towards the construction of a border wall found opposition in the courts, and only gained the green light from SCOTUS in mid-2019, with a later confirmation approved in 2020. Other action to revoke law enforcement grants to sanctuary cities faced trouble before judges, slowing the stride of the anti-invasion movement.

In the face of a porous border and other national threats, we cannot run the risk of actions being interrupted based on liberal quibbling and frivolous litigation. The answer lies with an important tool known as the "notwithstanding clause" which developed in Canada and was popularized for American readers by Robert Bork.[287] This device is designed to be attached to legislative acts and prevent their stalling by the judiciary over an initial period of five or so years. One can easily see the advantage of the method in relation to immigration restriction orders done on an executive basis. A conservative president could for instance authorize the transfer of funds to finish the border wall and block TPS acceptances while restricting legal counterattacks for a period of several years by use of a signing statement. Legal challenges might still be mounted, but any rulings would have to wait until the end of that period to go into effect, allowing the wall to be finished and a stemming of the migration flow to materialize.

Where court machinations become problematic, it is also possible to create more favorable conditions to reduce migration, particularly of the illegal variety. The president commands ultimate power over national defense priorities, and is permitted to act with great latitude in service of the public good. Who is to deny that the cartel issue in Mexico and its associated ripple effects are rising to the level of a national security threat? We already have seen almost 100 individuals on the terror watch list be apprehended while attempting to gain entry to America through the southern border.[288] More will probably come thanks to the loose border controls championed by both major parties in service to their corporate donors.

Americans can resist such madness by demanding full militarization of the borderland. Now, direct confrontation with the cartels and infiltrating terrorists could foreseeably create a saddening state of war, though of course the long-term impact must be balanced with other objectives. It does not imply conflict with the Mexican government specifically, but rather the deadly drug rings that prey on Mexican people and police in barbaric fashion. If circumstances become tense, migration will diminish temporarily, permitting completion of the border wall and the avoidance of smuggling tragedies. National authorities can then move to invoke the provisions of the REAL ID Act which bar entry by refugees who accepted "material support" from an organization deemed to be a "terrorist support group".[289] Strict interpretation of the clause applied to cartel organizations or "coyote" smugglers means a drastic drop in migration by definition, and expanding it to TPS applicants would work wonders for reducing numbers.

A point of reference regarding immigration of the legal variety is the prerogative to simply dismiss or not enforce laws which are determined by the president to be ill-founded or unconstitutional. Thomas Jefferson for instance did not bend before Supreme Court rulings in favor of the Alien and Sedition Acts, which were enacted by Federalist Party members to target their opponents in the Democratic-Republican coalition. Jefferson couched his opinion in the notion that all branches were independent and equal, and thus the judiciary could not have the final say on the punitive legislations. As he noted: "You seem to think it devolved on the judges to decide on the validity of the sedition law, [...] But nothing in the

Constitution has given them the right to decide for the Executive, more than the Executive to decide for them. Both magistracies are equally independent in the sphere of action assigned to them."[290] While Jefferson did not question the standing of the court in making its rulings on the laws, he elected to not enforce them and in fact rolled back the implications through his pardon power.

Other presidents have taken related actions. Andrew Jackson famously campaigned against the National Bank of the United States, citing in particular its 30 percent ownership by foreigners as an anathema to the nation's best interest.[291] He would adopt a line similar to Jefferson by emphasizing the co-equal nature of the branches and dismissing suggestions that judicial opinion could hamper the president's ability to act, even as the courts attempted to uphold the legal validity of the bank project: "The opinion of the judges has no more authority over Congress than the opinion of Congress has over judges. [...] on that point the president is independent of both."[292]

Franklin Roosevelt would employ similar logic when it came to the enforcement or interpretation of the Neutrality Acts, which he himself signed throughout the 1930s. In order to get around provisions blocking arms sales to European countries, FDR simply classified the materiel as "surplus" and succeeded in promulgating his soft interventionism to support Great Britain.[293] Roosevelt was malleable towards the concept of emergency action as well, arguing in his initial inaugural speech that, "our Constitution is so simple and practical that it is possible always to meet extraordinary needs by changes in emphasis and arrangement without loss of essential form."[294] The president went on to advocate an expansion of emergency powers over domestic affairs in the vein of the Executive protecting his country from foreign invasion.[295]

How might that angle be used towards immigration? Well, simply put, a conservative president should look to interpret immigration-related statutes such as the Hart-Celler Act of 1965 and the concurring 1990 Immigration Act from the lens of a national security and heritage-respecting position. Given that Hart-Cellar in particular was not designed to explicitly make large changes in demographics, its structures being largely color-blind in nature, diverting the focus will merely require a bit of legal wit on the part of the president. Chain migration in particular is the cause of the massive waves from Africa and Asia, so declining to enforce those provisions or shifting their allowance to Europe and South America is an obvious path forward to resetting the imbalanced population trends. Of course to be successful in this regard will require an overhaul of staffing at the USCIS to ensure that civil servants are not undermining the national mission.

A final area of presidential creativity concerns the 14th Amendment of the Constitution, which is popularly understood to award birthright citizenship to anyone who is born on American soil, regardless of their parents' citizenship status. In the earlier days of the country such a policy might have been reasonable due to lower population totals, but today it is subject to abuse, both by legal entrants and their undocumented compatriots. As with all other laws, whether supreme in nature or mere legislative acts, the amendment is open to interpretation. At stake is the section which reads as follows: "All persons born or naturalized in the United States and subject to the jurisdiction thereof, are citizens of the United States and of the State wherein they reside." The verbiage concerning jurisdiction is complicating, as following birthright citizenship to the letter would render it superfluous, like Edward Erler notes.[296] Indeed, the oft-cited 1898 case of Wong Kim Ark which forms the basis for *jus soli* (born on the soil) citizenship in the United States today was only decided by a 5-4 vote on the Supreme Court, with strong dissent from the incumbent chief justice. What remains to be tested is for a president to issue his understanding by executive fiat on the matter of birthright citizenship, and allow the legal process to play out. The present threats of birth tourism and illegal immigration could make a compelling argument for new interpretations, and success would mean the long-term protection of the homeland against mass immigration of all varieties.

While there is nothing wrong with non-Europeans as people, the American nation will not survive on the basis of some deracinated diversity bazaar serving the global elite. Traditions are more than mere paper; they embody a people with common ancestry and an ability to identify with the Founders, not see them through the filter of a social justice agenda fixated on the past existence of slavery. As Edmund Burke understood it, society is not made up merely of existing individuals, but involves a contract with past generations as well.[297] Consequently, we should make decisions that take into consideration what our forefathers would have thought, and maintain the image of the nation they built, rather than surrendering to the cheap appeals of globalism and neoliberal consumerism. By embracing this process we protect the "democracy of the dead",[298] a concept valuing tradition and ethnic heritage as the guiding lights of America's national story.

X. Closing Thoughts

It is probable that one of three primary reactions will be exhibited by readers of this book, especially if they are in the skeptical camp. The first is colored by those who feel the measures proposed go too far, per chance far enough until the system entirely becomes threatened. They opt instead for a "conservative" Conservatism, the same model of institutionalism we prosecuted earlier in the text. Here aspirants to political relevancy believe reticence and hesitation are more admirable paths, even if the outcome is a nation burning. To rid themselves from responsibility their fingers point at the Plural Left, arguing it is the other side taking damnation's path, and not conservatives. Providing Rightists do not join in the squalor, they are free to pass on with a smile to face, sleeping guiltless in eternal fashion.

But are we so resigned to death that the battle itself is not worth entering? Have suggestions of hand-tying prevailed upon us enough to care little of today, or the lives still unborn? A man can be excused for not acting when he is powerless, yet when the means are before him and he stalwart refuses to use them, only the label of cowardly traitor belongs fixed to his lapel. Sluggish tolerance and inaction are not reasonable responses to the national conundrum.

The second party's complaint is one of not being extreme enough. Forget using the system, they implore. We must simply toss it out in favor something completely new, filled with dynamism and promise. Younger souls in particular may amass around the suggestion because it feeds their frustration with the existing corruptions and insincerity native to modern politics. A single fell swoop will repair the damage done, preferably through total dictatorship or military and church domination.

In that case, fears of "what will it become" remain good stoppages. Armed uprisings are normally backed by some measure of elites, the military brass being no exception. Furthermore, we ought to demure on the prospect of defense contractors or oil companies becoming more controlling than they are today, pushing for wars to increase corporate profits. Legitimacy is another matter. Flawed as it may be, the Constitution holds currency in the minds of citizens with an enduring quality. Rotating to anything like a junta or single-person rule would rest credibility in them for only the duration of a natural life. What then happens if the leader dies, or the junta leaders age to gray? The system is bound to face a crisis which will likely lead to its total undoing because of a credibility loss. In the unfortunate event that a Leftist regime comes to power, there will be precious little to protect conservatives should constitutional guidelines be tossed out.

Lastly, choice spectators might agree with the measures proposed, but fear liberal electoral fraud will prevent the rise of another Rightist president. They can be assuaged by encouraging dynamic action at the state level, where election administration is situated. Since most fraud appears to occur in larger, Democratic Party-controlled cities, conservative legislators can enact laws which award electoral votes to the candidate who wins a majority of the state's counties. The effect would be clear nullification of the heavier population totals in urban areas and an expansion of democracy by making rural regions equally important, just as the Founders intended.

As we can now see, the middle path is the proper one to follow. It entails stanching the bleeding through sharp executive action so the nation can have a chance, both financially and in the realm of culture. When and while the salvation is ongoing, representatives can work through the amendment process to strengthen the Constitution and make it immune to left-wing tampering. Balanced budgets, sound money, and restoration of states' rights are at the core, but only once national objectives and resiliency have been secured.

Ultimately, we are called to cast ourselves on the stage of history, regardless of initial preference. The choice then is between fighting and retreating, demanding and accepting, life and expiration. If we are to build a better world for generations to come it must be based on courage and unswerving belief, not trembling hearts. One spirited stand against the ages, or an embittered ride across the River Styx.

References

Barr, W. P. (2022). *One Damn Thing After Another*. HarperCollins Publishers.

Benen, S. (2020). *The Imposters: How Republicans Quit Governing and Seized American Politics*. William Morrow.

Bolton, J. (2020). *The Room Where It Happened: A White House Memoir*. Simon and Schuster.

Bork, R. H. (2003). *Coercing Virtue: The Worldwide Rule of Judges*. The AEI Press.

Bork, R. H. (1996). *Slouching Towards Gomorrah*. ReganBooks.

Bradley, B. (1996). *Time Present, Time Past: A Memoir*. HarperCollins.

Burnham, J. (2014). *Suicide of the West: An Essay On the Meaning and Destiny of Liberalism*. Encounter Books.

Burnham, J. (2020). *The Machiavellians: Defenders of Freedom*. Lume Books.

Caldwell, C. (2020). *The Age of Entitlement: America Since the Sixties*. Simon & Schuster.

Chang, H. J. (2008). *Bad Samaritans: The Myth of Free Trade and the Secret History of Capitalism*. Bloomsbury Press.

Continetti, M. (2022). *The Right: The Hundred-Year War For American Conservatism*. Basic Books.

Cort, J. C. (1988). *Christian Socialism*. Orbis Books.

Corwin, E. S. (1977). *Presidential Power and the Constitution*. Ithaca, NY: Cornell University Press.

Crawford, A. (1980). *Thunder On The Right: The "New Right" and the Politics of Resentment*. Pantheon Books.

Disraeli, B. (1962). *Coningsby*. The New American Library.

D'Souza, D. (2018). *Death of a Nation: Plantation Politics and the Making of the Democratic Party*. All Points Books.

Emba, C. (2022). *Rethinking Sex: A Provocation*. Sentinel.

Emry, S., & Flinchpaugh, J. L. (2012). *Billions For The Bankers, Debts For The People*. J.L. Flinchpaugh
Publishing.

Flake, J. (2017). *Conscience of a Conservative: A Rejection of Destructive Politics and A Return To Principle*. Random House.

Francis, S. (1994). *Beautiful Losers: Essays on the Failures of American Conservatism*. University of Missouri.

Gessen, M. (2021). *Surviving Autocracy*. Riverhead Books.

Gibson, C. (2019). *El Norte: The Epic and Forgotten History of Hispanic North America*. Atlantic Monthly Press.

Goldberg, J. (2007). *Liberal Fascism: The Secret History of the American Left From Mussolini to the Politics of Meaning* . Doubleday.

Goldberg, M. (2020). *The Truth About Mussolini and Fascism*. Amazon Publishing

Goldwater, B. M., & Casserly, J. (1988). *Goldwater*. St. Martin's Press.

Gottfried, P. E., & Spencer, R. B. (2015). *The Great Purge: The Deformation of the Conservative Movement*. Washington Summit Publishers.

Gottfried, P. E. (2012). *Leo Strauss and The Conservative Movement in America: A Critical Appraisal*. Cambridge University Press.

Gottfried, P. E. (2020). *The Vanishing Tradition: Perspectives On American Conservatism*. Northern Illinois University Press.

Greenwald, G. (2008). *Great American Hypocrites: Toppling The Big Myths of Republican Politics*. Three Rivers Press.

Guerrero, J. (2020). *Hatemonger: Stephen Miller, Donald Trump, and the White Nationalist Agenda*. New York, NY: William Morrow, an imprint of HarperCollins.

Hanson, V. D. (2021). *The Dying Citizen: How Progressive Elites, Tribalism, and Globalization Are Destroying the Idea of America*. Basic Books.

Harvey, R. (2011). *Bolivar: The Liberator of Latin America*. Skyhorse Publishing.

Hayek, F. A. (1994). *The Road to Serfdom*. The University of Chicago Press.

Hayward, S. F. (2017). *Patriotism Is Not Enough: Harry Jaffa, Walter Berns, And The Arguments That Redefined American Conservatism*. New York, NY: Encounter Books.

Hicks, J. D. (1960). *Republican Ascendancy: 1921-1933*. Harper & Row Publishers.

Hitchens, P. (2008). *The Abolition of Britain: From Winston Churchill to Theresa May*. Bloomsbury Continuum.

Hyman, L. (2018). *Temp: How American Work, American Business, and the American Dream Became Temporary*. Viking Publishing.

Karl, J. (2021). *Betrayal: The Final Act of the Trump Show*. Dutton - Penguin Random House.

Kirchick, J. (2022). *Secret City: The Hidden History of Gay Washington*. Henry Holt and Co.

Kirk, R., & McClay, W. M. (2019). *Russell Kirk's Concise Guide to Conservatism*. Regnery Publishing.

Kirk, R. (2001). *The Conservative Mind: From Burke to Eliot* (7th ed.). Regnery Publishing Inc.

Klinenberg, E. (2012). Going Solo: The Extraordinary Rise and Surprising Appeal of Living Alone. New York, NY: The Penguin Press.

Kolko, G. (1963). *The Triumph of Conservatism: A Reinterpretation of American History, 1900-1916*. The Free Press.

Levin, J. (2020). *The Queen: The Forgotten Life Behind An American Myth*. Back Bay Books.

Lipset, S. M. (1963). *Political Man: The Social Bases of Politics*. Anchor Books.

Locke, J. (2012). *Two Treatises of Government*. The Federalist Papers Project.

Lofgren, M. (2012). *The Party Is Over: How Republicans Went Crazy, Democrats Became Useless, and the Middle Class Got Shafted*. Penguin Books.

Manvell, R., & Fraenkel, H. (2011). *Goering: The Rise and Fall of The Notorious Nazi Leader*. Skyhorse Publishing, Inc.

McElroy, W., & Perry, L. (1991). *Freedom, Feminism, and the State*. Independent Institute.

Mearsheimer, J. J., & Walt, S. M. (2007). *The Israel Lobby and U.S. Foreign Policy* . Farrar, Straus and Giroux.

Milkis, S. M. (1999). *Political Parties and Constitutional Government: Remaking American Democracy*. Baltimore, MD: Johns Hopkins University Press.

Mitchell, B. (1989). *Weak Link: The Feminization of the American Military*. Regnery Gateway.

Murray, D. (2005). *Neoconservatism: Why We Need It*. Social Affairs Unit.

Neustadt, R. E. (1990). *Presidential Power And The Modern Presidents: The Politics of Leadership From Roosevelt to Reagan*. New York, NY: Free Press.

Oakley, J. R. (1990). *God's Country: America in the Fifties*. Barricade Books.

Orchowski, M. S. (2015). *The Law That Changed the Face of America: The Immigration and Nationality Act of 1965*. Rowman & Littlefield.

Owens, C. (2020). *Blackout: How Black America Can Make Its Second Escape From The Democrat Plantation*. Threshold Editions.

Ramaswamy, V. (2021). *Woke, Inc.: Inside Corporate America's Social Justice Scam*. Center Street.

Reedy, G. E. (1970). *The Twilight of the Presidency*. New York, NY: The New American Library.

Regan, D. T. (1988). *For The Record: From Wall Street To Washington*. Harcourt Brace Jovanovich, Publishers.

Rothbard, M. N. (2007). *The Betrayal of the American Right*. Ludwig von Mises Institute.

Rubin, D. (2020). *Don't Burn This Book: Thinking for Yourself in an Age of Unreason*. Sentinel.

Santorum, R. (2006). *It Takes a Family: Conservatism and the Common Good*. Wilmington, DE: ISI Books.

Schmitt, C. (1996). *Concept of The Political*. (G. Schwab, Trans.). The University of Chicago Press.

Schmitt, C. (2014). *Dictatorship: From the Origin of the Modern Concept of Sovereignty to Proletarian Class Struggle*. (M. Hoelzl & G. Ward, Trans.). polity.

Schmitt, C. (2008). *The Leviathan In The State Theory of Thomas Hobbes: Meaning and Failure of a Political Symbol*. (G. Schwab & E. Hilfstein, Trans.). The University of Chicago Press.

Schmitt, C. (2005). *Political Theology: Four Chapters On The Concept of Sovereignty*. (G. Schwab, Trans.). The University of Chicago Press.

Scruton, R. (2017). *Conservatism: An Invitation to the Great Tradition*. St. Martin's Press.

Scruton, R. (2014). *How to be a Conservative*. Bloomsbury.

Skowronek, S., Dearborn, J. A., & King, D. S. (2021). *Phantoms of a Beleaguered Republic: The Deep State And The Unitary Executive*. New York, NY: Oxford University Press.

Smith, R. N. (1982). *Thomas E. Dewey and His Times*. New York, NY: Simon and Schuster.

Somoza, A., & Cox, J. (1980). *Nicaragua Betrayed*. Western Islands Publishers.

Sorel, G., & Jennings, J. (1999). *Reflections On Violence*. Cambridge University Press.

Sykes, C. J. (2018). *How The Right Lost Its Mind*. St. Martin's Griffin.

Tygiel, J. (2006). *Ronald Reagan and the Triumph of American Conservatism*. Pearson Longman.

Wallis, J. (2005). *God's Politics: Why the Right Gets It Wrong and The Left Doesn't Get It*. New York, NY: HarperSanFrancisco.

Weissmann, A. (2021). *Where Law Ends: Inside the Mueller Investigation*. New York, NY: Random House.

Wheelan, C. (2016). *Naked Money: A Revealing Look at Our Financial System*. W. W. Norton & Company Inc.

Yoo, J. (2009). *Crisis and Command: A History of Executive Power From George Washington to the Present*. New York, NY: Kaplan.

Yoo, J. (2020). *Defender In Chief: Donald Trump's Fight For Presidential Power*. All Points Books.

About the Author

Martin Goldberg is a social scientist and educator who has also authored the books *Centrism: Why We Need It, The Truth About Mussolini and Fascism,* and *Socialism of the Right.* He blogs at www.martingoldberg.net and is active elsewhere in the digital realm. When not putting pen to the word processor, he can be found working outdoors and developing an organic garden, somewhere in the South.

Notes

[1] Crawford, A. (1980). *Thunder On The Right: The "New Right" and the Politics of Resentment*. Pantheon Books. pg. 113.

[2] Disraeli, B. (1962). *Coningsby*. The New American Library. pp. 118-119.

[3] Kolko, G. (1963). *The Triumph of Conservatism: A Reinterpretation of American History, 1900-1916*. The Free Press. pp. 4, 59-65, 132-133, 292.

[4] Francis, S. (1994). *Beautiful Losers: Essays on the Failures of American Conservatism*. University of Missouri. pg. 105.

[5] Ibid, pg. 111.

[6] Crawford, A. (1980). *Thunder On The Right: The "New Right" and the Politics of Resentment*. Pantheon Books. pp. 229-234.

[7] Ibid, pg. 233.

[8] Ibid, pp. 231-232.

[9] Dickerson, J. (2016, May 12). *Never Goldwater: How the fight to defeat the Arizona senator gave birth to the modern GOP*. Slate Magazine. Retrieved October 2, 2022, from http://www.slate.com/articles/news_and_politics/politics/2016/05/never_goldwate r_the_failed_attempt_to_wrest_the_1964_gop_nomination_from.html

[10] Francis, S. (1994). *Beautiful Losers: Essays on the Failures of American Conservatism*. University of Missouri. pp. 61-72.

[11] Scruton, R. (2017). *Conservatism: An Invitation to the Great Tradition*. St. Martin's Press. pg. 9.

[12] Robinson, P., & Murray, D. (2020, December 1). *Douglas Murray and his continuing fight against the "Madness of Crowds"*. YouTube. Retrieved December 13, 2022, from https://www.youtube.com/watch?v=lp4XhZytdD0

[13] Hayek, F. A. (1994). *The Road to Serfdom*. The University of Chicago Press. pg. 66.

[14] Emba, C. (2022). *Rethinking Sex: A Provocation*. Sentinel. pg. 130.

[15] Bork, R. H. (1996). *Slouching Towards Gomorrah*. ReganBooks. pg. 63.

[16] Kaschuta, A., & Agent, A. (2022, May 25). *Academic agent - who rules US?* YouTube. Retrieved December 10, 2022, from https://www.youtube.com/watch?v=F7B28gJtOdQ

[17] Hitchens, P. (2008). *The Abolition of Britain: From Winston Churchill to Theresa May*. Bloomsbury Continuum. pg. 210.

[18] Bork, R. H. (1996). *Slouching Towards Gomorrah*. ReganBooks. pg. 25.

[19] Scruton, R. (2017). *Conservatism: An Invitation to the Great Tradition*. St. Martin's Press. pg. 27.

[20] Kirk, R. (2001). *The Conservative Mind: From Burke to Eliot* (7th ed.). Regnery Publishing Inc. pg. 482.

[21] Santorum, R. (2006). *It Takes a Family: Conservatism and the Common Good*. Wilmington, DE: ISI Books. pg. 56.

[22] Caldwell, C. (2020). *The Age of Entitlement: America Since the Sixties*. Simon & Schuster. pp. 6, 13-17.

[23] Hayek, F. A. (1994). *The Road to Serfdom*. The University of Chicago Press. pg. xxxvi.

[24] Francis, S. (1994). *Beautiful Losers: Essays on the Failures of American Conservatism*. University of Missouri. pg. 209.

[25] McGregor, J., Jan, T., & Hoyer, M. (2021, August 23). *Big business pledged nearly $50 billion for racial justice after George Floyd's death. where did the money go?* The Washington Post. Retrieved October 10, 2022, from https://www.washingtonpost.com/business/interactive/2021/george-floyd-corporate-america-racial-justice/

[26] Jagannathan, M. (2021, April 21). *How racial-equity donations surged - then fell - after George Floyd's killing*. MarketWatch. Retrieved October 10, 2022, from https://www.marketwatch.com/story/racial-equity-donations-soared-then-fell-in-the-months-after-george-floyds-murder-by-a-police-officer-11619037824

[27] Staff, A. P. (2021, March 12). *A look at big settlements in US police killings*. AP NEWS. Retrieved October 10, 2022, from https://apnews.com/article/shootings-police-trials-lawsuits-police-brutality-2380f38268a504ae689ad5b64b5de2e7

[28] Hickey, A. (2021, May 25). *One year after George Floyd's death, corporate America is still scrambling to hire chief diversity officers*. Business Insider. Retrieved October 10, 2022, from https://www.businessinsider.com/chief-diversity-officers-in-demand-after-george-floyds-death-2021-5

[29] Bork, R. H. (1996). *Slouching Towards Gomorrah*. ReganBooks. pg. 3.

[30] Ibid, pg. 3.

[31] Ibid, pp. 3-4.

[32] Robinson, P. (2021, November 3). *Victor Davis Hanson diagnoses the dying citizen*. YouTube. Retrieved December 11, 2022, from https://www.youtube.com/watch?v=BQSjO5-sSOY

[33] Burnham, J. (2014). *Suicide of the West: An Essay On the Meaning and Destiny of Liberalism*. Encounter Books. pp. 29-30.

[34] Scruton, R. (2017). *Conservatism: An Invitation to the Great Tradition*. St. Martin's Press. pg. 45.

[35] Ibid, pp. 44-45.

[36] Bradley, B. (1996). *Time Present, Time Past: A Memoir*. HarperCollins. pg. 52.

[37] Francis, S. T. (2016, June 21). *Dr. Samuel T. Francis - "Race and the American right" (American Renaissance Conference, 2000)*. YouTube. Retrieved October 10, 2022, from https://www.youtube.com/watch?v=E2eG0l52Au0

[38] Flake, J. (2017). *Conscience of a Conservative: A Rejection of Destructive Politics and A Return To Principle*. Random House. pg. x.

[39] Huetteman, E. (2022, August 27). *McCain hated Obamacare. He also saved it*. NBCNews.com. Retrieved August 7, 2022, from https://www.nbcnews.com/health/obamacare/mccain-hated-obamacare-he-also-saved-it-n904106

[40] Elving, R. (2017, July 26). *What is the 'regular order' John McCain longs to return to on Health Care?* NPR. Retrieved September 25, 2022, from https://www.npr.org/2017/07/26/539358654/what-is-the-regular-order-john-mccain-longs-to-return-to-on-health-care

[41] Pergam, A. (2009, December 18). *Funny-guy-turned-senator Al Franken Disses Lieberman*. NBC Connecticut. Retrieved August 7, 2022, from

https://www.nbcconnecticut.com/news/local/funny-guy-turned-senator-al-franken-disses-lieberman/1859493/

[42] Hanson, V. D. (2021). *The Dying Citizen: How Progressive Elites, Tribalism, and Globalization Are Destroying the Idea of America*. Basic Books. pp. 17, 237-239.

[43] Oakley, J. R. (1990). *God's Country: America in the Fifties*. Barricade Books. pp. 156-157.

[44] Mimms, G. (2018, November 13). *Ronald Reagan's 1983 amendments to the Social Security Act of 1935*. SeniorInfo4U. Retrieved August 7, 2022, from http://www.seniorinfo4u.com/blog/ronald-reagans-1983-amendments-to-the-social-security-act-of-1935/

[45] WeAreSocialSecurity. (2012, November 5). *Ronald Reagan: "Social Security has nothing to do with the deficit."*. YouTube. Retrieved August 7, 2022, from https://www.youtube.com/watch?v=ihUoRD4pYzI

[46] Page, B. R. (2019, November 5). *Revisions to revenue projections suggest that the TCJA cost more than expected*. Tax Policy Center. Retrieved August 8, 2022, from https://www.taxpolicycenter.org/taxvox/revisions-revenue-projections-suggest-tcja-cost-more-expected

[47] Staff, P. R. (2018, April 19). Mitch McConnell backs out of trump plan to cut $60 billion in spending. ThePalmieriReport. Retrieved August 8, 2022, from https://thepalmierireport.com/mitch-mcconnell-backs-out-of-trump-plan-to-cut-60-billion-in-spending/

[48] Chappell, B. (2020, June 1). *Protesting racism versus risking COVID-19: 'I wouldn't weigh these crises separately'*. NPR. Retrieved October 23, 2022, from https://www.npr.org/sections/coronavirus-live-updates/2020/06/01/867200259/protests-over-racism-versus-risk-of-covid-i-wouldn-t-weigh-these-crises-separate

[49] Barr, W. P. (2022). *One Damn Thing After Another*. HarperCollins Publishers. pp. 59, 125-126, 488-489.

[50] Stewart, P. (2020, June 7). *Trump wanted to deploy 10,000 troops in Washington D.C., official says*. Reuters. Retrieved October 23, 2022, from https://www.reuters.com/article/us-minneapolis-police-protest-troops/trump-wanted-to-deploy-10000-troops-in-washington-d-c-official-says-idUSKBN23E0DY

[51] Karl, J. (2021). *Betrayal: The Final Act of the Trump Show*. Dutton - Penguin Random House. pg. 41.

[52] Martin, M., & Ermyas, T. (2022, May 9). *Former Pentagon chief Esper says Trump asked about shooting protesters*. NPR. Retrieved October 23, 2022, from https://www.npr.org/2022/05/09/1097517470/trump-esper-book-defense-secretary

[53] Bump, P. (2022, May 2). *Analysis | Donald Trump's dangerous view of state violence*. The Washington Post. Retrieved October 23, 2022, from https://www.washingtonpost.com/politics/2022/05/02/donald-trumps-dangerous-view-state-violence/

[54] Staff, A. (2020, June 4). *Defense secretary catches White House off guard with opposition to military use, photo op*. Axios. Retrieved October 23, 2022, from https://www.axios.com/2020/06/03/mark-esper-insurrection-act-protests

[55] Barr, W. P. (2022). *One Damn Thing After Another*. HarperCollins Publishers.

pg. 503.

[56] Olson, T. (2020, June 1). *Barr: Violence from Antifa, other groups 'is domestic terrorism and will be treated accordingly'*. Fox News. Retrieved December 21, 2022, from https://www.foxnews.com/politics/barr-george-floyd-violence-from-antifa-other-group-is-domestic-terrorism-and-will-be-treated-accordingly

[57] Ibid, pp. 488-489.

[58] Robinson, P. (2022). *More Than "One Damn Thing," with Bill Barr. YouTube/ More Than "One Damn Thing," with Bill Barr*. The Hoover Institute. Retrieved October 301, 2022, from https://www.youtube.com/watch?v=q1oeJwF5tG4. Approx. 23:20 timestamp.

[59] Barr, W. P. (2022). *One Damn Thing After Another*. HarperCollins Publishers. pp. 504-505.

[60] Hermann, P., & Hsu, S. S. (2020, September 1). *Prosecutor accuses D.C. police of making rioting arrests with insufficient evidence*. The Washington Post. Retrieved October 30, 2022, from https://www.washingtonpost.com/local/public-safety/prosecutor-accuses-dc-police-of-making-rioting-arrests-with-insufficient-evidence/2020/09/01/96310954-ec61-11ea-99a1-71343d03bc29_story.html

[61] Robinson, P. (2022). *More Than "One Damn Thing," with Bill Barr. YouTube/ More Than "One Damn Thing," with Bill Barr*. The Hoover Institute. Retrieved October 301, 2022, from https://www.youtube.com/watch?v=q1oeJwF5tG4. Approx. 1:01:00 timestamp.

[62] Sorel, G., & Jennings, J. (1999). *Reflections On Violence*. Cambridge University Press. pg. 61.

[63] Ibid, pp. 61-63.

[64] Schmitt, C. (1996). *Concept of The Political*. (G. Schwab, Trans.). The University of Chicago Press. pg. 47.

[65] Gessen, M. (2021). *Surviving Autocracy*. Riverhead Books. pp. 10-11.

[66] Schmitt, C. (2005). *Political Theology: Four Chapters On The Concept of Sovereignty*. (G. Schwab, Trans.). The University of Chicago Press. pg. xiii.

[67] Ibid, pg. xlvii.

[68] Somoza, A., & Cox, J. (1980). *Nicaragua Betrayed*. Western Islands Publishers. pp. 298-301.

[69] Olson, W. (2020, December 29). *Trump Cannot Stay In Power By Declaring Martial Law*. Cato.org. Retrieved October 30, 2022, from https://www.cato.org/blog/trump-cannot-stay-power-declaring-martial-law

[70] Schmitt, C. (2014). *Dictatorship: From the Origin of the Modern Concept of Sovereignty to Proletarian Class Struggle*. (M. Hoelzl & G. Ward, Trans.). polity. pp. 149-151.

[71] Woodruff Swan, B. (2020, March 21). *DOJ seeks new emergency powers amid coronavirus pandemic*. POLITICO. Retrieved October 30, 2022, from https://www.politico.com/news/2020/03/21/doj-coronavirus-emergency-powers-140023

[72] Cheney, L. (2021, May 12). *Opinion | Liz Cheney: The GOP is at a turning point. history is watching us*. The Washington Post. Retrieved December 12, 2022, from https://www.washingtonpost.com/opinions/2021/05/05/liz-cheney-republican-party-turning-point/

[73] Regan, D. T. (1988). *For The Record: From Wall Street To Washington*.

Harcourt Brace Jovanovich, Publishers. pp. 283-285.

[74] Faux, J. (2013, December 9). *NAFTA's impact on U.S. workers*. Economic Policy Institute. Retrieved August 28, 2022, from https://www.epi.org/blog/naftas-impact-workers/

[75] Vlahos, K. B. (2015, March 25). *CAFTA reinvigorates job-loss issue*. Fox News. Retrieved August 29, 2022, from https://www.foxnews.com/story/cafta-reinvigorates-job-loss-issue

[76] Scott, R. E. (2015, March 17). *What's wrong with the TPP? this deal will lead to more job loss and downward pressures on the wages of most working Americans*. Economic Policy Institute. Retrieved August 29, 2022, from https://www.epi.org/blog/whats-wrong-with-the-tpp-this-deal-will-lead-to-more-job-loss-and-downward-pressures-on-the-wages-of-most-working-americans/

[77] Keck, Z. (2014, October 28). *Rand Paul to Obama: Finish TPP trade deal*. The Diplomat. Retrieved August 29, 2022, from https://thediplomat.com/2014/10/rand-paul-to-obama-finish-tpp-trade-deal/

[78] Stein, J. (2017, January 23). *Paul Ryan used to Love TPP. then came Donald Trump*. Vox. Retrieved August 29, 2022, from https://www.vox.com/policy-and-politics/2017/1/23/14359196/paul-ryan-trump-tpp

[79] Vinopal, C. (2019, December 11). *These 4 changes helped Trump and Democrats agree to the USMCA trade deal*. PBS. Retrieved August 30, 2022, from https://www.pbs.org/newshour/economy/making-sense/these-4-changes-helped-trump-and-democrats-agree-to-the-usmca-trade-deal

[80] Guillen, M. (2016, September 6). *NAFTA's impact on the U.S. economy: What are the facts?* Knowledge at Wharton. Retrieved September 1, 2022, from https://knowledge.wharton.upenn.edu/article/naftas-impact-u-s-economy-facts/#:~:text=For%20all%20that%2C%20most%20studies,trade%20growth%20fostered%20by%20NAFTA.

[81] Jones, C. (2022, February 1). *Where have the manufacturing jobs gone as U.S. factories closed?* USA Today. Retrieved September 4, 2022, from https://www.usatoday.com/story/money/2022/02/01/manufacturing-jobs-factory-closings/9298274002/

[82] Dean, A., & Kimmel, S. (2019). Free trade and opioid overdose death in the United States. *SSM - population health, 8*, 100409. https://doi.org/10.1016/j.ssmph.2019.100409

[83] Youssef, S., & Rector, R. (1999, May 11). *The determinants of welfare caseload decline*. The Heritage Foundation. Retrieved September 5, 2022, from https://www.heritage.org/welfare/report/the-determinants-welfare-caseload-decline

[84] Danielson, C., & Klerman, J. A. (2008). Did Welfare Reform Cause the Caseload Decline? *Social Service Review, 82*(4), 703–730. https://doi.org/10.1086/597347

[85] Haskins, R. (2016, July 28). *Welfare Reform, success or failure? it worked*. Brookings. Retrieved September 5, 2022, from https://www.brookings.edu/articles/welfare-reform-success-or-failure-it-worked/

[86] Haskins, R., Albert, V., & Howard, K. (2016, July 28). *The responsiveness of the Temporary Assistance for Needy Families Program during the Great*

Recession. Brookings. Retrieved September 5, 2022, from https://www.brookings.edu/research/the-responsiveness-of-the-temporary-assistance-for-needy-families-program-during-the-great-recession/

[87] Staff, B. G. (2009, February 2). *Welfare rolls decline even as economy falls.* Boston.com. Retrieved September 5, 2022, from http://archive.boston.com/news/nation/washington/articles/2009/02/02/welfare_rolls_decline_even_as_economy_falls/

[88] Deparle, J. (2012, April 8). *Welfare limits left poor adrift as recession hit.* The New York Times. Retrieved September 5, 2022, from https://www.nytimes.com/2012/04/08/us/welfare-limits-left-poor-adrift-as-recession-hit.html

[89] Plumer, B. (2021, November 25). *Why are 47 million Americans on food stamps? it's the recession - mostly.* The Washington Post. Retrieved September 5, 2022, from https://www.washingtonpost.com/news/wonk/wp/2013/09/23/why-are-47-million-americans-on-food-stamps-its-the-recession-mostly/

[90] Staff, R. (2011, February 10). *Obama budget has $2.5 billion cut in heat aid for poor.* Reuters. Retrieved September 5, 2022, from https://www.reuters.com/article/us-usa-budget-heating/obama-budget-has-2-5-billion-cut-in-heat-aid-for-poor-idUSTRE71902D20110210

[91] Fay, B. (2020, November 17). *Obama's budget would change how Social Security Colas are calculated.* Debt.org. Retrieved September 5, 2022, from https://www.debt.org/blog/obamas-budget-seeks-to-cut-social-security/

[92] Benen, S. (2020). *The Imposters: How Republicans Quit Governing and Seized American Politics.* William Morrow. pp. 217-218.

[93] Rosenbaum, D., & Keith-Jennings, B. (2019, June 6). *Snap caseload and spending declines have accelerated in recent years.* Center on Budget and Policy Priorities. Retrieved September 5, 2022, from https://www.cbpp.org/research/food-assistance/snap-caseload-and-spending-declines-have-accelerated-in-recent-years

[94] Schnell, L., & Hughes, T. (2019, December 29). *'a terrible time to be poor': Cuts to snap benefits will hit 700,000 Hungry Americans.* USA Today. Retrieved September 5, 2022, from https://www.usatoday.com/story/news/nation/2019/12/21/trump-food-stamps-cut-snap-benefits-more-hungry-americans/2710146001/

[95] Goldstein, A. (2021, August 10). *Welfare rolls decline during the pandemic despite economic upheaval.* The Washington Post. Retrieved September 5, 2022, from https://www.washingtonpost.com/health/2021/08/01/welfare-roles-during-the-pandemic/

[96] Dreyfus, H. (2021, December 29). States are hoarding $5.2 billion in welfare funds even as the need for aid grows. ProPublica. Retrieved September 5, 2022, from https://www.propublica.org/article/states-are-hoarding-52-billion-in-welfare-funds-even-as-the-need-for-aid-grows

[97] Lee, M. Y. H. (2021, December 7). *Analysis | do 'welfare' recipients get $35,000 in benefits a year?* The Washington Post. Retrieved September 5, 2022, from https://www.washingtonpost.com/news/fact-checker/wp/2014/12/05/grothman-single-parents-welfare/

[98] Pao, M. (2015, November 19). *How america's child support system failed to*

keep up with the Times. NPR. Retrieved September 5, 2022, from
https://www.npr.org/2015/11/19/456632896/how-u-s-parents-racked-up-113-
billion-in-child-support-debt

[99] Sorensen, E., & Oliver, H. (2002, February 1). *Child Support Reforms in PRWORA: Initial Impacts*. Assessing the New Federalism. Retrieved September 5, 2022, from https://www.urban.org/sites/default/files/publication/60361/410421-Child-Support-Reforms-in-PRWORA.PDF

[100] Goldberg, M. (2020). *The Truth About Mussolini and Fascism*. Amazon Publishing . pp. 59-63.

[101] Wall, T. (2015, March 30). *Businesses take a stand against Indiana's religious freedom restoration act*. Inc.com. Retrieved September 11, 2022, from https://www.inc.com/thompson-wall/indianas-new-religious-freedom-act-deterring-big-business.html

[102] Swiatek, J., & Evans, T. (2015, March 31). *9 ind.. CEOS call for changes to 'religious freedom' law*. USA Today. Retrieved September 11, 2022, from https://www.usatoday.com/story/money/business/2015/03/30/ind-religious-freedom-bill-business-reaction/70693326/

[103] McBride, S., & Durso, L. E. (2018, November 1). *Indiana's religious freedom restoration act is bad for business*. Center for American Progress. Retrieved September 11, 2022, from https://www.americanprogress.org/article/indianas-religious-freedom-restoration-act-is-bad-for-business/

[104] Bender, A. (2016, January 31). *Indiana's religious freedom act cost Indianapolis $60 million in lost revenue*. Forbes. Retrieved September 11, 2022, from https://www.forbes.com/sites/andrewbender/2016/01/31/indianas-religious-freedom-act-cost-indianapolis-60-million-in-lost-revenue/?sh=3aeeb2792e2a

[105] Cook, T. (2014, March 25). *Gov. Mike Pence signs off on business tax cuts*. The Indianapolis Star. Retrieved September 11, 2022, from https://www.indystar.com/story/news/politics/2014/03/25/gov-mike-pence-sign-business-tax-cuts/6859237/

[106] Caldwell, C. (2020). *The Age of Entitlement: America Since the Sixties*. Simon & Schuster. pp. 149-151.

[107] Sopelsa, B. (2016, July 9). *Major corporations join fight against North Carolina's 'bathroom bill'*. NBCNews.com. Retrieved September 11, 2022, from https://www.nbcnews.com/feature/nbc-out/major-corporations-join-fight-against-north-carolina-s-bathroom-bill-n605976

[108] Abadi, M. (2016, September 21). *North Carolina has lost a staggering amount of money over its controversial 'bathroom law'*. Business Insider. Retrieved September 11, 2022, from https://www.businessinsider.com/north-carolina-hb2-economic-impact-2016-9

[109] Staff, A. P. (2017, March 27). *'Bathroom bill' to cost North Carolina $3.76 billion*. CNBC. Retrieved September 11, 2022, from https://www.cnbc.com/2017/03/27/bathroom-bill-to-cost-north-carolina-376-billion.html

[110] Gottfried, P. E. (2020). *The Vanishing Tradition: Perspectives On American Conservatism*. Northern Illinois University Press. pg. 33.

[111] Ibid, pg. 42.

[112] Ibid, pg. 31.

113 Ibid, pg. 35.
114 Regan, D. T. (1988). *For The Record: From Wall Street To Washington*. Harcourt Brace Jovanovich, Publishers. pg. 296.
115 Manvell, R., & Fraenkel, H. (2011). *Goering: The Rise and Fall of The Notorious Nazi Leader*. Skyhorse Publishing, Inc. pg. 151.
116 Oakley, J. R. (1990). *God's Country: America in the Fifties*. Barricade Books. pp. 70-71.
117 Gottfried, P. E. (2020). *The Vanishing Tradition: Perspectives On American Conservatism*. Northern Illinois University Press. pp. 102-108.
118 Stacker. (2022, May 31). *California is the #7 state with the most land owned by the Federal Government*. FOX 5 San Diego. Retrieved February 12, 2023, from https://fox5sandiego.com/news/california-news/california-is-the-7-state-with-the-most-land-owned-by-the-federal-government/
119 Fuhrman, J. (2018). The Hidden Dangers of Fast and Processed Food*. American Journal of Lifestyle Medicine, 12(5), 375–381. https://doi.org/https://www.ncbi.nlm.nih.gov/pmc/articles/PMC6146358/
120 Rapaport, L. (2019, June 5). *More evidence links ultra-processed foods to health harms*. Reuters. Retrieved February 12, 2023, from https://www.reuters.com/article/us-health-diet-processed-food/more-evidence-links-ultra-processed-foods-to-health-harms-idUSKCN1T61YX
121 Kirchick, J. (2022). *Secret City: The Hidden History of Gay Washington*. Henry Holt and Co. pg. 142.
122 Ibid, pg. 157.
123 Ibid, pg. 163.
124 Ibid, pg. 441.
125 Ibid, pp. 365-368.
126 Ibid, pg. 560.
127 Gottfried, P. E., & Spencer, R. B. (2015). *The Great Purge: The Deformation of the Conservative Movement*. Washington Summit Publishers. pg. xvii.
128 Vogue, A. de. (2015, June 26). *Roberts issues stern dissent in same-sex marriage case | CNN politics*. CNN. Retrieved June 27, 2022, from https://www.cnn.com/2015/06/26/politics/john-roberts-gay-marriage-dissent/index.html
129 McCullough, J. J. (2018, May 9). *Time for a compromise on transgenderism*. National Review. Retrieved December 26, 2022, from https://www.nationalreview.com/2018/05/transgenderism-compromise-necessary-to-preserve-social-order/
130 Owens, C. (2020). *Blackout: How Black America Can Make Its Second Escape From The Democrat Plantation*. Threshold Editions. pg. 93.
131 McGraw, M. (2021, August 16). *The GOP waves white flag in the same-sex marriage wars*. POLITICO. Retrieved June 27, 2022, from https://www.politico.com/news/2021/08/16/republicans-gay-marriage-wars-505041
132 Schnell, M. (2022, July 20). *These are the 47 House Republicans who voted for a bill protecting marriage equality*. The Hill. Retrieved July 31, 2022, from https://thehill.com/homenews/house/3566600-these-are-the-47-house-republicans-

who-voted-for-a-bill-protecting-marriage-equality/

[133] Gerstein, J., & Ward, A. (2022, May 2). *Exclusive: Supreme Court has voted to overturn abortion rights, draft opinion shows*. POLITICO. Retrieved December 12, 2022, from https://www.politico.com/news/2022/05/02/supreme-court-abortion-draft-opinion-00029473

[134] McElroy, W., & Perry, L. (1991). *Freedom, Feminism, and the State*. Independent Institute. pp. 167-168.

[135] Hyman, L. (2018). *Temp: How American Work, American Business, and the American Dream Became Temporary*. Viking Publishing. pp. 51-66.

[136] Toossi, M., & T. L. (2017, July). Women In The Workforce Before, During, And After The Great Recession. Retrieved from https://www.bls.gov/spotlight/2017/women-in-the-workforce-before-during-and-after-the-greatrecession/pdf/women-in-the-workforce-before-during-and-after-the-great-recession.pdf

[137] Klinenberg, E. (2012). Going Solo: The Extraordinary Rise and Surprising Appeal of Living Alone. New York, NY: The Penguin Press. pg. 75.

[138] Silverstein, M. J., & Sayre, K. (2015, July 16). The Female Economy. Harvard Business Review. Retrieved September 18, 2022, from https://hbr.org/2009/09/the-female-economy

[139] Staff, C. (2021, December 8). *Buying power (quick take)*. Catalyst. Retrieved September 19, 2022, from https://www.catalyst.org/research/buying-power/

[140] Maier, M. (2015, September 18). *Women Consumers Control 85% of spending power*. Luce Performance Group. Retrieved September 19, 2022, from https://www.luceperformancegroup.com/Women-Consumers-Control-85-percent-Of-Spending-Power___635774267810750931_blog.htm

[141] Miller, C. C. (2016, March 18). *As women take over a male-dominated field, the pay drops*. The New York Times. Retrieved September 19, 2022, from https://www.nytimes.com/2016/03/20/upshot/as-women-take-over-a-male-dominated-field-the-pay-drops.html

[142] Mitchell, B. (1989). *Weak Link: The Feminization of the American Military*. Regnery Gateway. pg. 131.

[143] Ibid, pp. 131-143.

[144] Staff, eM. M. W. (2001, September 20). *Text: President Bush Addresses the Nation*. The Washington Post. Retrieved September 20, 2022, from https://www.washingtonpost.com/wp-srv/nation/specials/attacked/transcripts/bushaddress_092001.html

[145] Garcia, F. (2016, November 17). *US state bill could make hijabs and niqabs illegal in public*. The Independent. Retrieved September 20, 2022, from https://www.independent.co.uk/news/world/americas/georgia-hijab-niqab-ban-illegal-bill-islam-muslims-law-a7423441.html

[146] D'Souza, D. (2018). *Death of a Nation: Plantation Politics and the Making of the Democratic Party*. All Points Books. pp. 35-37.

[147] Ramaswamy, V. (2021). *Woke, Inc.: Inside Corporate America's Social Justice Scam*. Center Street. pp. 294-295.

[148] Bork, R. H. (1996). *Slouching Towards Gomorrah*. ReganBooks. pg. 298.

[149] Hayward, S. F. (2017). *Patriotism Is Not Enough: Harry Jaffa, Walter Berns, And The Arguments That Redefined American Conservatism*. New York, NY:

Encounter Books. pp. 112-113.

[150] D'Souza, D. (2018). *Death of a Nation: Plantation Politics and the Making of the Democratic Party*. All Points Books. pp. 103-111.

[151] Ibid, pp. 22, 171-173.

[152] Ibid, pp. 26-28, 267-272.

[153] Ibid, pp. 15-16.

[154] Ibid, pg. 60.

[155] Waxman, O. B. (2017, January 25). *Donald Trump picks Andrew Jackson portrait for Oval Office*. Time. Retrieved August 8, 2022, from https://time.com/4649081/andrew-jackson-donald-trump-portrait/

[156] D'Souza, D. (2018). *Death of a Nation: Plantation Politics and the Making of the Democratic Party*. All Points Books. pp. 142-145.

[157] Orchowski, M. S. (2015). The Law That Changed the Face of America: The Immigration and Nationality Act of 1965. Rowman & Littlefield. pg. 38.

[158] Milkis, S. M. (1999). Political Parties and Constitutional Government: Remaking American Democracy. Baltimore, MD: Johns Hopkins University Press. pp. 92-98.

[159] Ibid, pg. 98.

[160] Oakley, J. R. (1990). *God's Country: America in the Fifties*. Barricade Books. pg. 376.

[161] Milkis, S. M. (1999). Political Parties and Constitutional Government: Remaking American Democracy. Baltimore, MD: Johns Hopkins University Press. pg. 117.

[162] Ibid, pp. 164-165.

[163] Oakley, J. R. (1990). *God's Country: America in the Fifties*. Barricade Books. pp. 340, 376.

[164] Ibid, pp. 191-195.

[165] Ibid, pg. 194.

[166] Ibid, pg. 376.

[167] Gottfried, P. E., & Spencer, R. B. (2015). *The Great Purge: The Deformation of the Conservative Movement*. Washington Summit Publishers. pp. xvi-xvii.

[168] Continetti, M. (2022). *The Right: The Hundread-Year War For American Conservatism*. Basic Books. pg. 128.

[169] Levin, J. (2020). *The Queen: The Forgotten Life Behind An American Myth*. Back Bay Books. pg. 90.

[170] Hayward, S. F. (2017). *Patriotism Is Not Enough: Harry Jaffa, Walter Berns, And The Arguments That Redefined American Conservatism*. New York, NY: Encounter Books. pg. 123.

[171] Goldberg, J. (2007). *Liberal Fascism: The Secret History of the American Left From Mussolini to the Politics of Meaning* . Doubleday. pg. 232.

[172] D'Souza, D. (2018). *Death of a Nation: Plantation Politics and the Making of the Democratic Party*. All Points Books. pp. 204-208.

[173] Goldwater, B. M., & Casserly, J. (1988). Goldwater. St. Martin's Press. pg. 246.

[174] Ibid, pp. 216-217.

[175] Hayward, S. F. (2017). *Patriotism Is Not Enough: Harry Jaffa, Walter Berns, And The Arguments That Redefined American Conservatism*. New York, NY:

Encounter Books. pg. 182.

[176] Kirk, R. (2001). *The Conservative Mind: From Burke to Eliot* (7th ed.). Regnery Publishing Inc. pp. iv-v.

[177] Hanson, V. D. (2021). *The Dying Citizen: How Progressive Elites, Tribalism, and Globalization Are Destroying the Idea of America.* Basic Books. pp. 65-69.

[178] Ibid, pg. 71.

[179] Brinton, S. (2020, July 10). *Was Teddy Roosevelt a racist? You decide.* Long Island Herald. Retrieved June 19, 2022, from https://www.liherald.com/stories/was-teddy-roosevelt-a-racist-you-decide,126499

[180] Hanson, V. D. (2021). *The Dying Citizen: How Progressive Elites, Tribalism, and Globalization Are Destroying the Idea of America.* Basic Books. pg. 100.

[181] Ibid, pp. 101-105.

[182] Cillizza, C., & Cohen, J. (2012, November 8). *President Obama and the White Vote? no problem.* The Washington Post. Retrieved June 20, 2022, from https://www.washingtonpost.com/news/the-fix/wp/2012/11/08/president-obama-and-the-white-vote-no-problem/

[183] Tygiel, J. (2006). *Ronald Reagan and the Triumph of American Conservatism.* Pearson Longman. pg. 117.

[184] Walshe, S. (2013, March 18). *RNC Completes 'Autopsy' on 2012 Loss, Calls for Inclusion Not Policy Change.* ABC News. Retrieved August 22, 2022, from https://abcnews.go.com/Politics/OTUS/rnc-completes-autopsy-2012-loss-calls-inclusion-policy/story?id=18755809

[185] Watson, K. (2018, February 24). *Former RNC chair responds to comment about his race and position.* CBS News. Retrieved August 8, 2022, from https://www.cbsnews.com/news/former-rnc-chair-responds-to-comment-about-his-race-and-position/

[186] Williams, T. D. (2022, July 16). *Catholic League: Black leadership joins White Supremacists on abortion.* Breitbart. Retrieved August 8, 2022, from https://www.breitbart.com/faith/2022/07/15/catholic-league-black-leadership-sides-with-white-supremacists-over-abortion/

[187] Williams, T. (2022, August 29). *Catholic League: White Liberals are the real 'white supremacists'.* Breitbart. Retrieved August 30, 2022, from https://www.breitbart.com/faith/2022/08/29/catholic-league-white-liberals-are-real-white-supremacists/

[188] Setyon, J. (2018, September 19). *Virginia Republican announces Senate campaign to protest Corey Stewart.* Reason.com. Retrieved August 18, 2022, from https://reason.com/2018/09/19/virginia-republican-announces-senate-cam/

[189] McIntosh, B. (2022, January 20). *Youngkin appoints new director of diversity and inclusion.* WSET. Retrieved August 18, 2022, from https://wset.com/news/local/angela-sailor-governor-glenn-youngkin-appoints-new-director-of-diversity-and-inclusion

[190] Murray, Delaney. "Attorney General Miyares Creates 'First of Its Kind' Antisemitism Task Force for Virginia." *WRIC ABC 8News*, WRIC ABC 8News, 10 Feb. 2023, https://www.wric.com/news/virginia-news/attorney-general-miyares-creates-first-of-its-kind-antisemitism-task-force-for-virginia.

[191] Staff, C. (n.d.). *How groups voted in 2020.* How Groups Voted in 2020 | Roper

Center for Public Opinion Research. Retrieved December 15, 2022, from https://ropercenter.cornell.edu/how-groups-voted-2020

[192] Bork, R. H. (1996). *Slouching Towards Gomorrah*. ReganBooks. pp. 228, 240.

[193] Orchowski, M. S. (2015). The Law That Changed the Face of America: The Immigration and Nationality Act of 1965. Rowman & Littlefield. pp. 35-36.

[194] Ibid, pg. 22.

[195] Ibid, pg. 78.

[196] Ibid, pp. 76-77.

[197] Ibid, pg. 75.

[198] Ibid, pp. 40, 74.

[199] Ibid, pp. 75-76.

[200] Ibid, pg. 83.

[201] *Immigration and nationality act of 1965*. US House of Representatives: History, Art & Archives. (n.d.). Retrieved November 27, 2022, from https://history.house.gov/Historical-Highlights/1951-2000/Immigration-and-Nationality-Act-of-1965/#:~:text=The%20law%20capped%20the%20number,of%20the%20family%20reunification%20clause.

[202] Orchowski, M. S. (2015). *The Law That Changed the Face of America: The Immigration and Nationality Act of 1965*. Rowman & Littlefield. pg. 81.

[203] Kammer, J. (2018, August 2). *Three decades of failed reform: Immigration politics and the collapse of Worksite Enforcement*. CIS.org. Retrieved November 27, 2022, from https://cis.org/Oped/Three-Decades-Failed-Reform-Immigration-Politics-and-Collapse-Worksite-Enforcement

[204] Ibid.

[205] Orchowski, M. S. (2015). *The Law That Changed the Face of America: The Immigration and Nationality Act of 1965*. Rowman & Littlefield. pg. 84.

[206] Ibid, pg. 79.

[207] Ainsley, J. (2022, October 22). *Migrant border crossings in Fiscal Year 2022 topped 2.76 million, breaking previous record*. NBCNews.com. Retrieved November 27, 2022, from https://www.nbcnews.com/politics/immigration/migrant-border-crossings-fiscal-year-2022-topped-276-million-breaking-rcna53517

[208] Walsh, D. (2006, April 12). *Immigration bill may lose felony proviso*. CNN. Retrieved November 28, 2022, from https://edition.cnn.com/2006/POLITICS/04/11/immigration/index.html?section=cnn_us

[209] Staff, N. I. L. C. (2006, May 30). *Senate approves CIR of 2006*. National Immigration Law Center. Retrieved November 28, 2022, from https://www.nilc.org/issues/immigration-reform-and-executive-actions/cir-06/

[210] Kammer, J. (2018, August 2). Three decades of failed reform: Immigration politics and the collapse of Worksite Enforcement. CIS.org. Retrieved November 27, 2022, from https://cis.org/Oped/Three-Decades-Failed-Reform-Immigration-Politics-and-Collapse-Worksite-Enforcement

[211] Anderson, S. (2020, July 21). *Trump cuts legal immigrants by half and he's not done yet*. Forbes. Retrieved November 28, 2022, from https://www.forbes.com/sites/stuartanderson/2020/07/21/trump-cuts-legal-

immigrants-by-half-and-hes-not-done-yet/?sh=3a9f40a06168

[212] Marcos, C. (2017, June 29). *House passes 'Kate's law' and Bill Targeting Sanctuary Cities*. The Hill. Retrieved November 28, 2022, from https://thehill.com/blogs/floor-action/house/340137-house-passes-kates-law-and-crackdown-on-sanctuary-cities/

[213] Lee, M. (2020, December 4). *Senate passes Bill Fighting Immigration Discrimination and protecting American workers*. Senate Passes Bill Fighting Immigration Discrimination and Protecting American W... Retrieved November 28, 2022, from https://www.lee.senate.gov/2020/12/senate-passes-bill-fighting-immigration-discrimination-and-protecting-american-workers

[214] Smith, R. N. (1982). *Thomas E. Dewey and His Times*. New York, NY: Simon and Schuster. pp. 427-429.

[215] Rothbard, M. N. (2007). *The Betrayal of the American Right*. Ludwig von Mises Institute. pp. 122-126.

[216] Ibid, pp. 125-126.

[217] Ibid, pp. 86-87.

[218] Ibid, pp. 123, 168-169, 188-189.

[219] Schultz, C. (2013, March 18). *Nixon prolonged Vietnam War for political gain-and Johnson knew about it, newly unclassified tapes suggest*. Smithsonian.com. Retrieved November 13, 2022, from https://www.smithsonianmag.com/smart-news/nixon-prolonged-vietnam-war-for-political-gainand-johnson-knew-about-it-newly-unclassified-tapes-suggest-3595441/

[220] Continetti, M. (2022). *The Right: The Hundread-Year War For American Conservatism*. Basic Books. pp. 224-225.

[221] Mearsheimer, J. J., & Walt, S. M. (2007). *The Israel Lobby and U.S. Foreign Policy* . Farrar, Straus and Giroux. pg. 288.

[222] Ibid, pg. 288.

[223] Ibid, pp. 288-289.

[224] Ibid, pg. 288.

[225] Ibid, pg. 242.

[226] Ibid, pg. 246.

[227] Ibid, pg. 240.

[228] Greenwald, G. (2008). *Great American Hypocrites: Toppling The Big Myths of Republican Politics*. Three Rivers Press. pg. 120.

[229] Ibid, pp. 130-131.

[230] Mearsheimer, J. J., & Walt, S. M. (2007). *The Israel Lobby and U.S. Foreign Policy* . Farrar, Straus and Giroux. pg. 152.

[231] Staff, A. P. (2011, October 18). *Paul wants to end aid to Israel*. Boston.com. Retrieved November 14, 2022, from http://archive.boston.com/news/local/massachusetts/articles/2011/10/18/paul_wants_to_end_aid_to_israel/

[232] Mearsheimer, J. J., & Walt, S. M. (2007). *The Israel Lobby and U.S. Foreign Policy* . Farrar, Straus and Giroux. pg. 301.

[233] Woolf, N., & Holpuch, A. (2015, January 21). *John Boehner invites Netanyahu to address Congress on Iran next month*. The Guardian. Retrieved November 14, 2022, from https://www.theguardian.com/us-news/2015/jan/21/boehner-

netanyahu-invite-congress-iran-obama
[234] Clifton, E. (2014, November 4). *Exclusive: Emergency Committee For Israel Spends Big On Rep. Cotton*. LobeLog. Retrieved November 14, 2022, from https://lobelog.com/exclusive-emergency-committee-for-israel-spends-big-on-rep-tom-cotton/
[235] Pink, A. (2017, May 2). *Texas becomes 17th state to pass law outlawing BDS*. The Forward. Retrieved November 15, 2022, from https://forward.com/fast-forward/370725/texas-becomes-17th-state-to-pass-law-outlawing-bds/
[236] Greenwald, G. (2018, December 17). *A Texas Elementary School speech pathologist refused to sign a pro-israel oath, now mandatory in many states - so she lost her job*. The Intercept. Retrieved November 15, 2022, from https://theintercept.com/2018/12/17/israel-texas-anti-bds-law/
[237] Haberman, M. (2022, May 5). *Trump proposed launching missiles into Mexico to 'destroy the drug labs,' Esper says*. The New York Times. Retrieved December 19, 2022, from https://www.nytimes.com/2022/05/05/us/politics/mark-esper-book-trump.html
[238] Goldwater, B. M., & Casserly, J. (1988). *Goldwater*. St. Martin's Press. pg. 21.
[239] Flake, J. (2017). *Conscience of a Conservative: A Rejection of Destructive Politics and A Return To Principle*. Random House. pg. xi.
[240] Ibid, pp. 55-56.
[241] Continetti, M. (2022). *The Right: The Hundred-Year War For American Conservatism*. Basic Books. pg. 136.
[242] Sykes, C. J. (2018). *How The Right Lost Its Mind*. St. Martin's Griffin. pg. 228.
[243] Ibid, pp. xviii-xix.
[244] Flake, J. (2017). *Conscience of a Conservative: A Rejection of Destructive Politics and A Return To Principle*. Random House. pp. 111-114.
[245] Wessel, D. (2022, March 9). What is reconciliation in Congress? Brookings. Retrieved October 12, 2022, from https://www.brookings.edu/blog/up-front/2021/02/05/what-is-reconciliation-in-congress/
[246] Delaney, A. (2022, July 27). *Democrats outsmart Mitch McConnell with surprise reconciliation deal*. Yahoo! News. Retrieved October 12, 2022, from https://news.yahoo.com/mitch-mcconnell-scheme-thwart-democrats-015029531.html?guccounter=1&guce_referrer=aHR0cHM6Ly93d3cuZ29vZ2xlL mNvbS8&guce_referrer_sig=AQAAANHUyonVu_TeKqwbeT8rnglxSyFfHh6By SGgokB5rB_2LgrrX3FOyQAyhR_xn8H-YhdcidZxembRmLm5pNkUCBNds_vU2bITx1TMXogOk5Sm3nVags6REUKUF 6CZ_CRX0mmfQHzZGYzQLd798or_9ucqQKN3hE-II8sc6Yeff6lV
[247] Burnham, J. (2020). *The Machiavellians: Defenders of Freedom*. Lume Books. pg. 37.
[248] Ibid, pg. 47.
[249] Ibid, pg. 48.
[250] Ibid, pp. 47-49.
[251] Schmitt, C. (2014). *Dictatorship: From the Origin of the Modern Concept of Sovereignty to Proletarian Class Struggle*. (M. Hoelzl & G. Ward, Trans.). polity. pp. 16-17.
[252] Healy, G. (2007, July 5). Conservatives and the Presidency. Cato.org. Retrieved

September 25, 2022, from https://www.cato.org/blog/conservatives-presidency
[253] Lipset, S. M. (1963). *Political Man: The Social Bases of Politics*. Anchor Books. pg. 64.
[254] Schmitt, C. (2014). *Dictatorship: From the Origin of the Modern Concept of Sovereignty to Proletarian Class Struggle*. (M. Hoelzl & G. Ward, Trans.). polity. pp. 32-33.
[255] Locke, J. (2012). *Two Treatises of Government*. The Federalist Papers Project. pg. 159.
[256] Yoo, J. (2009). *Crisis and Command: A History of Executive Power From George Washington to the Present*. New York, NY: Kaplan. pp. 20-21.
[257] Ibid, pg. 3.
[258] Ibid, pp. 22-23.
[259] Ibid, pg. 123.
[260] Duignan, B. (2022, February 12). *Executive order 11905*. Encyclopædia Britannica. Retrieved October 18, 2022, from https://www.britannica.com/event/Executive-Order-11905
[261] Kravets, D. (2013, February 5). *Obama's memo on targeted killings is a drone strike on the law*. Wired. Retrieved October 18, 2022, from https://www.wired.com/2013/02/legal-basis-killing-americans/
[262] Totenberg, N. (2020, June 18). *Supreme Court rules for dreamers, against trump*. NPR. Retrieved October 18, 2022, from https://www.npr.org/2020/06/18/829858289/supreme-court-upholds-daca-in-blow-to-trump-administration
[263] Stern, M. J. (2019, June 27). *John Roberts rejects the census citizenship question because trump officials lied about it*. Slate Magazine. Retrieved October 18, 2022, from https://slate.com/news-and-politics/2019/06/supreme-court-census-citizenship-question-roberts.html
[264] Jost, T. S. (2022, January 24). *The Supreme Court weighs in on vaccine mandates*. Commonwealth Fund. Retrieved October 18, 2022, from https://www.commonwealthfund.org/blog/2022/supreme-court-weighs-vaccine-mandates
[265] Skowronek, S., Dearborn, J. A., & King, D. S. (2021). *Phantoms of a Beleaguered Republic: The Deep State And The Unitary Executive*. New York, NY: Oxford University Press. pg. 153.
[266] Ibid, pg. 153.
[267] Ibid, pp. 155-157.
[268] Guerrero, J. (2020). *Hatemonger: Stephen Miller, Donald Trump, and the White Nationalist Agenda*. New York, NY: William Morrow, an imprint of HarperCollins. pp. 205-207.
[269] Dawsey, J., Eilperin, J., Hudson, J., & Rein, L. (2020, November 14). *In Trump's final days, a 30-year-old aide purges officials seen as insufficiently loyal*. The Washington Post. Retrieved November 2, 2022, from https://www.washingtonpost.com/politics/trump-white-house-purge/2020/11/13/2af12c94-25ca-11eb-8672-c281c7a2c96e_story.html
[270] Freedman, D. H. (2022, October 26). *Sweet Revenge: What trump would do in a second term*. Newsweek. Retrieved October 30, 2022, from https://www.newsweek.com/2022/11/04/sweet-revenge-what-trump-would-do-

second-term-1754654.html
[271] Oakley, J. R. (1990). *God's Country: America in the Fifties*. Barricade Books. pp. 71-72.
[272] Skowronek, S., Dearborn, J. A., & King, D. S. (2021). Phantoms of a Beleaguered Republic: The Deep State And The Unitary Executive. New York, NY: Oxford University Press. pp. 27-33.
[273] Ibid, pg. 26.
[274] Ibid, pg. 25.
[275] Yoo, J. (2020). *Defender In Chief: Donald Trump's Fight For Presidential Power*. All Points Books. pp. 14-15.
[276] Yoo, J. (2009). *Crisis and Command: A History of Executive Power From George Washington to the Present*. New York, NY: Kaplan. pg. xv.
[277] Skowronek, S., Dearborn, J. A., & King, D. S. (2021). Phantoms of a Beleaguered Republic: The Deep State And The Unitary Executive. New York, NY: Oxford University Press. pp. 183-184.
[278] Bolton, J. (2020). *The Room Where It Happened: A White House Memoir*. Simon and Schuster. pp. 488-489.
[279] Taibbi, M. (2019, January 16). *Has the government legalized secret defense spending?* Rolling Stone. Retrieved January 23, 2023, from https://www.rollingstone.com/politics/politics-features/secret-government-spending-779959/
[280] Wheelan, C. (2016). *Naked Money: A Revealing Look at Our Financial System*. W. W. Norton & Company Inc. pp. 135-151.
[281] Emry, S., & Flinchpaugh, J. L. (2012). *Billions For The Bankers, Debts For The People*. J.L. Flinchpaugh
Publishing. pp. 54-55.
[282] Ibid, pp. 65-66.
[283] Guerrero, J. (2020). *Hatemonger: Stephen Miller, Donald Trump, and the White Nationalist Agenda*. New York, NY: William Morrow, an imprint of HarperCollins. pp. 224-229.
[284] Skowronek, S., Dearborn, J. A., & King, D. S. (2021). *Phantoms of a Beleaguered Republic: The Deep State And The Unitary Executive*. New York, NY: Oxford University Press. pp. 144-146.
[285] Gibson, C. (2019). *El Norte: The Epic and Forgotten History of Hispanic North America*. Atlantic Monthly Press. pp. 369-371.
[286] Raia, P. (2022, October 10). *DeSantis aims to stop foreign buyers of Real Estate*. Hernando Sun. Retrieved November 6, 2022, from https://www.hernandosun.com/2022/10/10/desantis-aims-to-stop-foreign-buyers-of-real-estate/
[287] Bork, R. H. (2003). *Coercing Virtue: The Worldwide Rule of Judges*. The AEI Press. pp. 90-91.
[288] Giaritelli, A. (2022, October 25). *Nearly 100 FBI terror watchlist suspects nabbed at Southern Border*. Washington Examiner. Retrieved November 26, 2022, from https://www.washingtonexaminer.com/policy/defense-national-security/nearly-100-fbi-terror-watch-list-suspects-caught-southern-border
[289] Orchowski, M. S. (2015). *The Law That Changed the Face of America: The*

Immigration and Nationality Act of 1965. Rowman & Littlefield. pp. 88-89.
[290] Yoo, J. (2009). *Crisis and Command: A History of Executive Power From George Washington to the Present*. New York, NY: Kaplan. pp. 106-107.
[291] Chang, H. J. (2008). *Bad Samaritans: The Myth of Free Trade and the Secret History of Capitalism*. Bloomsbury Press. pp. 92-93.
[292] Yoo, J. (2009). *Crisis and Command: A History of Executive Power From George Washington to the Present*. New York, NY: Kaplan. pg. 166.
[293] Ibid, pg. 297.
[294] Ibid, pg. 262.
[295] Ibid, pp. 262-263.
[296] Erler, E. J. (2019, August 23). *Trump's critics are wrong about the 14th amendment and birthright citizenship*. National Review. Retrieved November 6, 2022, from https://www.nationalreview.com/2015/08/birthright-citizenship-not-mandated-by-constitution/
[297] Scruton, R. (2017). *Conservatism: An Invitation to the Great Tradition*. St. Martin's Press. pp. 30-31.
[298] Kirk, R., & McClay, W. M. (2019). *Russell Kirk's Concise Guide to Conservatism*. Regnery Publishing. pp. 10-11.